U. S. Department of Justice

Federal Bureau of Prisons

I0468778

LEGAL RESOURCE GUIDE

TO THE

FEDERAL BUREAU OF PRISONS

2014

Table of Contents

I. INTRODUCTION...1
    A. The Bureau's Mission..2
    B. This Publication...2
    C. Website...2
    D. District of Columbia (D.C.) Code Felony Offenders.................................2

II. PRETRIAL ISSUES..3
    A. Pretrial Detention...3
    B. Pretrial Inmate Health Care...3

III. EVALUATION OF OFFENDER MENTAL CAPACITY 4
    A. Pretrial: Mental Evaluation and Commitment:
       Title 18   U.S.C. § 4241   4
    B. Pretrial: Determination of Insanity at Time of Offense and Commitment:
       Title 18 U.S.C. §§ 4242 and 4243 5
    C. Conviction and Pre-Sentencing Stage:
       Title 18 U.S.C. § 4244 6
    D. Post-Sentencing Hospitalization:
       Title 18 U.S.C. § 4245 6
    E. Hospitalization of Mentally Incompetent Person Due for Release:
       Title 18 U.S.C. § 4246 7
    F. Civil Commitment of a Sexually Dangerous Person:
       Title 18 U.S.C. § 4248 7
    G. Examination of an Inmate Eligible for Parole:
       Title 18 U.S.C. § 4205 8
    H. Presentence Study and Psychological or Psychiatric   Examination:
       Title 18 U.S.C. § 3552(b) and (c)...8
    I. State Custody; Remedies in Federal Courts:
       Title 28 U.S.C. § 2254;
       Prisoners in State Custody Subject to Capital Sentence:
       Appointment of Counsel;   Requirement of Rule of Court or Statute;
       Procedures for Appointment:
       Title 28 U.S.C. § 2261..9

IV. SENTENCING ISSUES
    A. Probation and Conditions of Probation 9
       1. Community Confinement...9
       2. Intermittent Confinement..10
       3. Home Detention 10
    B. Imprisonment...10
       1. Institutional Confinement..10
       2. Service of Sentence in Non-Federal Facilities 10

    3. Juvenile Offenders 11
  C. Judgment in a Criminal Case...11
    1. Judicial Recommendations for a Specific Institution, Geographic Area, or
        Specialized Program..12
    2. Sentence Calculation...12
    3. Commencement of a Term of Imprisonment 12
    4. Credit for Prior Custody ("Jail Time")..13
    5. Credit for Satisfactory Behavior ("Good Conduct Time") 13
    6. Fines and Costs of Confinement 14
    7. Inmate Financial Responsibility Program 15

V. POST CONVICTION ISSUES..16
  A. Designation to a Facility for Service of a Term of Imprisonment 16
    1. Security Designation and Custody Classification......................................16
    2. DNA Collection..17
    3. Transportation to a Designated Institution..17
    4. Interstate Agreement on Detainers. 17
    5. Central Inmate Monitoring System 18
    6. Communication Management Units..18
    7. Special Management Units..19

  B. Admission and Orientation Program for Inmates...19

  C. Programs and General Services..19
    1. Education and Recreation Programs 19
    2. Religious Programs 20
    3. Food Service..21
    4. Work Programs and UNICOR 21
    5. Inmate Accident Compensation 22
        (a) Lost-Time Wage Program 22
        (b) Compensation for Work-Related Physical Impairment or Death........22
    6. Female Offenders...22
        (a) Birth Control and Pregnancy 23
        (b) Abortion...23
    7. Substance Abuse Treatment..24
    8. Urine Surveillance Program 24
    9. Medical Services 25
        (a) Medical Services Available to Sentenced Offenders.......................25
        (b) Medical Referral Centers 26
        (c) Voluntary Mental Health and Medical Treatment...........................27
        (d) Managing Infectious Disease 28
    10. Mental Health Counseling and Treatment Services....................................28
        (a) Involuntary Mental Health Treatment. 28
        (b) Mental Health Programs..29

         (c)   Sex Offender Management and Treatment...29

         (d)   Implementation of the Prison Rape Elimination Act of 2003...........30

         (e)   Treatment of Inmates with Gender Dysphoria 30

  D. Visiting, Telephones, and Correspondence..31

      1. Visiting...31

      2. Telephones 31

      3. Written and Electronic Correspondence 32

  E. Inmate Discipline Procedure...32

  F. Inmate Access to Court...33

      1. Law Libraries 33

      2. Preparation of Legal Documents..33

      3. Attorneys 34

      4. Legal Mail 34

      5. Unmonitored Legal Telephone Calls 34

      6. Inmate Involvement in Litigation While Incarcerated 35

  G. Administrative Remedy Program...36

  H. Personal Property 37

  I. Inmate Liens..38

  J. Special Administrative Measures..38

      1. National Security Cases 38

      2. Prevention of Acts of Violence and Terrorism 39

  K. Family Emergencies and Temporary Releases 39

      1. Furloughs..39

      2. Escorted Trips 40

  L. Release 40

      1. Early Release from Prison..40

         (a)   Executive Clemency 40

         (b)   Reduction in Sentence 40

      2. Parole.. 41

      3. Community Confinement...41

      4. Home Confinement 42

  M. Notification to Community of the Release of an Offender............................43

VI.   CONCLUSION 44

VII.   APPENDICES

Appendix A - Summary Table:

Application of Title18 U.S.C. Ch. 313: Offenders with Mental Disease or Defect. 45

Appendix B - Regional Counsel and Consolidated Legal Center offices 49

Appendix C - Relevant Acronyms and Abbreviations... 52

I. INTRODUCTION

The Federal Bureau of Prisons (Bureau or BOP), an agency of the United States Department of Justice (DOJ), was established in 1930 to provide more progressive and humane care for federal inmates, to professionalize the prison service, and to ensure consistent and centralized administration of the 11 federal prisons in operation at that time. Today, the BOP consists of more than 119 institutions, six Regional Offices, a Central Office (headquarters) located in Washington, D.C., a Designation and Sentence Computation Center (DSCC) located in Grand Prairie, Texas, two staff training centers, and 22 Residential Reentry Management (RRM) Offices. Regional Offices and the Central Office provide administrative oversight and support to the institutions and RRMs. The DSCC completes designations and sentence computations for the majority of inmates in BOP custody; the Office of Medical Designations and Transportation (OMDT) will assign those inmates with specific medical needs. RRMs oversee Residential Reentry Centers (RRCs) and home confinement programs. Inmates may be designated to any one of a number of Bureau of Prisons facilities: a United States Penitentiary (USP); a Federal Correctional Institution (FCI); a Federal Medical Center (FMC); a Federal Prison Camp (FPC) ; a Federal Detention Center (FDC); an Administrative Maximum Facility (ADX); or to a contract facility. Often, institutions with varied security levels, are co-located, at a Federal Correctional Complex (FCC).

The BOP is responsible for the custody and care of sentenced federal inmates as well as a significant number of pretrial detainees and pre-sentenced offenders housed in our facilities on behalf of the United States Marshals Service (USMS). The BOP also has custodial responsibility for District of Columbia felons sentenced to terms of imprisonment, and houses a number of state and military offenders on a contractual basis. The current inmate population exceeds 218,000 men and women, housed in both federal prisons and in private facilities under contract with the BOP. Approximately 28,000 inmates are housed in 15 major contract facilities under the oversight of the BOP Privatization Management Branch.

Federal Prison Industries (trade name "UNICOR") and the National Institute of Corrections are components of the BOP. UNICOR is managed by a Board of Directors, and the Director of the BOP serves as Chief Executive Officer.   Created by Congress in 1934, this wholly-owned government corporation provides inmates with needed prison employment and the opportunity to learn marketable skills. Items produced in UNICOR factories are sold to government agencies nationwide.   Many BOP institutions house a UNICOR factory or service.

The National Institute of Corrections (NIC), established in 1974, provides training, technical assistance, information services and cooperative agreement awards to service provider groups, and will directly assist state and local corrections agencies.   The NIC Director and 16-member Advisory Board, appointed by the Attorney General, advise assistance strategies and manage the Institute's funding priorities.

BOP contracts with private firms with correctional expertise to operate prisons to house felony offenders, predominantly criminal aliens, who might otherwise be incarcerated in BOP facilities. The contractor is required to adhere to most BOP policies for offender management, and has day-to-day operations responsibility, with general oversight by the BOP Privatization Management Branch.

A. The Bureau's Mission

The mission of the Bureau of Prisons is to protect society by confining offenders in the controlled environment of prisons and community-based facilities that are safe, humane, cost-efficient and appropriately secure, and to provide work and other self-improvement opportunities to assist offenders in becoming law-abiding citizens.

The federal prison system is the largest correctional system in the United States and continues to grow at a rate of approximately 2.6% per year. Most crimes in this country are committed by recidivists. With approximately 50,000 to 60,000 inmates released from federal prisons back to U.S. communities each year, reentry is a critical element of the mission of the BOP.

The Bureau's longstanding philosophy regarding reentry is that preparation for reentry begins on the first day of incarceration. To support reentry efforts, the Bureau has changed its focus from an emphasis on clinical assessment and program participation to a competency-based model that measures success by skill acquisition and ultimately successful community transition.

B. This Publication

This publication is intended to serve as a guide to relevant statutes, regulations, policy documents, and current case law concerning issues the BOP faces today.   It provides a general overview of the BOP, its services, and its programs. Statutes, regulations, case law and agency policies (Program Statements), referred to in this Guide may have been changed since publication. Thus, readers are advised to review the website and confirm cited legal references when exploring BOP matters. BOP legal staff are located in Regional Counsel's offices, and in Consolidated Legal Centers (CLCs) servicing individual institutions (see Appendix B).   Further inquiries may be directed to the appropriate CLC.

C. Website

The BOP Internet home page is located at www.bop.gov.   Consult the site for population data, policies, a directory of BOP facilities and offices, inmate locator information, employment opportunities, directions for inquiries under the Freedom of Information Act, and links to other relevant internet sites. The site for the National Institute of Corrections is www.nicic.gov. UNICOR's site is www.UNICOR.gov.

D. District of Columbia (D.C.) Code Felony Offenders

By virtue of Section 11201 of Chapter 1 of Subtitle C of Title XI of the National Capital Revitalization and Self-Government Improvement Act of 1997 (Revitalization Act), enacted August 5, 1997, Pub. L. No. 105-33, the BOP administers the imprisonment terms of felony offenders convicted under the D.C. criminal code. The BOP has broad authority to provide for the "custody, care, subsistence, education, treatment and training" of D.C. Code felony offenders in its custody "consistent with the sentence[s] imposed." D.C. Code § 24-1201(a), (b). With few exceptions, BOP manages D.C. Code offenders no differently from U.S. Code offenders.

II. PRETRIAL ISSUES

A. Pretrial Detention

The BOP and USMS cooperate to manage the allocation of federal detention bed space. Ordinarily, pretrial inmates may be detained at BOP detention centers, and at other BOP facilities pending prosecution and/or sentencing. The USMS acquires detention bed space through agreements with state and local governments, and contracts with private vendors, in addition to the available BOP pretrial cells. The development of necessary detention resources in key districts, while emphasizing appropriately structured community supervision alternatives for non-violent offenders, is the primary focus of this cooperative effort. To the extent practicable, pretrial inmates are separated from sentenced inmates, in accordance with 18 U.S.C. § 3142(i)(2). Should a court have concerns about conditions of confinement, access to medical care, or any other issue relating to a defendant's pre-trial detention in a BOP facility, the BOP requests the opportunity to address such concerns prior to the issuance of a court order. See Pretrial Inmates, 28 C.F.R. pt. 551, subpt. J; Program Statement 7331.04, Pretrial Inmates. Parties raising such issues tend to seek injunctive release in the form of an order compelling or directing the custodian of the detainee to affirmatively act in some way or refrain from action. As the Warden or other custodian is not a party to the criminal prosecution, the government attorney litigating the matter is urged to contact the Warden or the BOP legal office advising the affected institution for assistance in factual development and litigation support.

B. Pretrial Inmate Health Care

Pretrial detainees held in BOP institutions are provided medical care on site by BOP staff and contractors. The USMS is responsible for the costs associated with medical care provided in the local community and the transportation of pretrial inmates in its custody, and will contract for community medical providers as necessary to address the needs of inmates held in non-BOP facilities.

There is virtually no health care issue of a defendant that would preclude subsequent commitment of the defendant to a federal institution. Medical care is available in all BOP facilities. Male inmates whose health care needs exceed those services available in a typical institution may be transferred to a BOP Medical Referral Center in Springfield, Missouri; Rochester, Minnesota; Butner, North Carolina; Lexington, Kentucky; or Devens, Massachusetts. Female inmates will be transferred to the Carswell Medical Referral Center in Fort Worth, Texas. Should an inmate require more specialized care, the inmate is sent to an appropriate community facility.

Specialized health care for sentenced inmates is also available at a number of BOP institutions and all institutions are wheelchair accessible. See infra, Section V - Post Conviction Issues, Medical Services.

III. EVALUATION OF OFFENDER MENTAL CAPACITY

In 1984, as part of a major sentencing reform effort, Congress enacted comprehensive provisions addressing the evaluation and treatment of mentally ill offenders. Title 18 U.S.C. Chapter 313, §§ 4241-4247, describes necessary judicial procedures which must be followed when an offender appears to be, or is, currently suffering from a mental disease or defect. See 28 C.F.R pt. 549, subpt. C; Program Statements 5310.12, Psychology Services Manual; 5310.13, Mentally Ill Inmates, Institution Management of; 6010.03, Psychiatric Evaluation and Treatment; and 6340.04, Psychiatric Services. The Adam Walsh Child Protection and Safety Act of 2006 (Walsh Act), Pub. L. No. 109-248, provides for the civil commitment of a sexually dangerous person subsequent to the completion of the term of incarceration, as codified in § 4248. Further detail is provided below. A Summary Table of the application of the following statutes, under Chapter 313, is attached as Appendix A.

Evaluations may be performed by an outside (non-BOP) psychologist or psychiatrist by specifically designating that condition in the Study order. If the defendant is housed in a BOP facility, a judge may designate in the order that an outside psychologist or psychiatrist be admitted into the facility to conduct the examination. If the defendant is housed in a local non-BOP facility, a judge may simply designate in the order that an outside psychologist or psychiatrist be admitted into that local non-BOP facility to conduct the examination. The designated mental health professional must contact the institution in advance to arrange admission into the facility to examine the inmate and avoid unnecessary delays. A court-ordered study conducted by a community psychologist or psychiatrist is a far quicker and less costly process. If an MRC placement is required, the statutory timeline does not begin until the inmate is received at the designated facility for evaluation.

A. Title 18 U.S.C. Section 4241:
Pretrial: Mental Evaluation and Commitment

Title 18 U.S.C. § 4241 explains the procedures necessary to determine the mental competency of a defendant at any time after the commencement of prosecution, and prior to sentencing. Should there be reasonable cause to question the defendant's competency, the court will order a hearing upon the motion of one of the parties, or upon its own motion. See 18 U.S.C. § 4241(a). Prior to the hearing, the court may order the defendant to undergo a psychiatric or psychological examination. See 18 U.S.C. § 4241(b). BOP has specially trained forensic psychologists and limited psychiatric resources, so such evaluation orders should reference a psychological evaluation or a psychiatric evaluation but only when absolutely necessary.

The court may commit the defendant to the custody of the Attorney General for placement in a suitable facility[1] to be examined for a reasonable period not to exceed 30 days, unless the director of the examining facility requests a reasonable extension, not to exceed 15 days. See 18 U.S.C. § 4247(b). After the examination period expires, a report is filed with the court by the facility's staff, and copies are provided to counsel. The BOP strongly encourages the court to have the initial § 4241 evaluation conducted by outside non-BOP mental health professionals. This can be accomplished by designating the outside specialist in the study order.

Following the hearing, if the court finds by a preponderance of the evidence that the defendant is mentally incompetent, the court must commit the defendant to the custody of the Attorney General for hospitalization and treatment in a suitable facility. This commitment period is for a reasonable period of time, not to exceed four months, to evaluate if there is a substantial probability that, in the foreseeable future, restoration of competency will result. See 18 U.S.C. § 4241(d)(1).[2]

An additional commitment period may be ordered if the charges have not been disposed of, and the court determines there is a substantial probability that the defendant will become competent to stand trial in the foreseeable future. See 18 U.S.C. § 4241(d)(2). The defendant cannot, however, be committed for a determination of his or her competency to stand trial for a period longer than the maximum possible sentence he or she faces. See United States v. DeBellis, 649 F.2d 1 (1st Cir. 1981). If the defendant becomes competent to stand trial during the examination period, the director of the examining facility files a certificate with the court stating such. A second competency hearing is held and, if the defendant is shown to be competent by a preponderance of the evidence, the prosecution resumes. See 18 U.S.C. § 4241(e).

B.   Title 18 U.S.C. Sections 4242 and 4243:
Pretrial: Determination of Insanity at Time of Offense and Commitment

Pursuant to 18 U.S.C. § 4242, the prosecuting attorney, after receiving notice that the defendant intends to rely upon the defense of insanity, may ask the court to order the defendant to undergo a psychological or psychiatric examination. Similar to a § 4241 study as described above, the § 4242 study may be conducted locally or, where incarceration is deemed necessary, at a BOP facility. After the issue of insanity has been raised, the fact finder is required to reach a special verdict of guilty; not guilty; or not guilty only by reason of insanity.

When an offender has been found not guilty only by reason of insanity, a hearing will be conducted no later than 40 days after the special verdict. See 18 U.S.C. § 4243(c). At the hearing, a person

---

[1]In addition to BOP and USMS contract facilities, 18 U.S.C. § 4247(i)(A) authorizes the Attorney General to contract with states, localities, political subdivisions, or private agencies for the confinement, hospitalization, or treatment of a person committed pursuant to 18 U.S.C. Chapter 313.

[2]The Supreme Court has held that the government may, in some circumstances, involuntarily administer antipsychotic drugs to a mentally ill defendant facing serious criminal charges in order to render the defendant competent to stand trial. See Sell v. United States, 539 U.S. 166 (2003).

found not guilty solely by reason of insanity has the burden of proving by clear and convincing evidence that his or her release would not create a substantial risk of bodily injury to another person or serious damage to the property of another. See 18 U.S.C. § 4243(d). Note that while the hearing *must* take place within 40 days, § 4247(b) states that the examination under § 4243 *may not exceed* 45 days. If the offender fails to meet the evidentiary standard, he or she will be committed to the custody of the Attorney General.

Once the offender has been committed, the Attorney General will make continuous reasonable efforts to release the offender to the state in which the offender was domiciled or tried, if the state will assume responsibility for his or her custody, care, and treatment. The Attorney General has authority to stipulate the terms and conditions under which a federal insanity acquittee will be placed in state custody for care and treatment. See 18 U.S.C. § 4243(e). There is a continuing federal interest in the inmate's state placement or conditional release, and any transferred individual cannot be unconditionally released by the state facility without the concurrence of the committing court. Accordingly, prior to discharge, the director of the state facility must first comply with 18 U.S.C. § 4243(f), and notify the committing court of the potential release. The federal court, applying federal standards, decides whether the acquittee will, in fact, be discharged.

C. Title 18 U.S.C. Section 4244:
 Conviction and Pre-Sentencing Stage:
 Mental Condition Prior to Time of Sentencing

If a defendant is found guilty of an offense, but a question is raised as to his or her mental condition prior to sentencing, the court may order a hearing and a mental examination to determine whether the defendant is presently suffering from a mental disease or defect such that commitment to a suitable facility for care or treatment, in lieu of imprisonment, is appropriate. See 18 U.S.C. § 4244. If, after the hearing, the court finds by a preponderance of the evidence that such placement is appropriate, the defendant will be provisionally sentenced to the maximum term authorized by law and committed to the custody of the Attorney General for hospitalization in a suitable facility. See 18 U.S.C. § 4244(d). If the defendant later recovers to the extent that he or she is no longer in need of care and treatment, the defendant will proceed to final sentencing. The court then has the option of modifying the provisional sentence. While the statute envisions "commitment in lieu of imprisonment," the § 4244 defendant actually faces an indeterminate period of commitment to a suitable facility for care or treatment; whereas, if he or she proceeds to final sentencing, there will be a definite term of imprisonment imposed, and the opportunity under § 4245 to receive necessary treatment.

D. Title 18 U.S.C. Section 4245:
 Post-Sentencing Hospitalization

Title 18 U.S.C. § 4245 provides for hospitalization and treatment of sentenced inmates found to be suffering from a mental disease or defect. If an inmate refuses to consent to hospitalization for care and treatment, § 4245 describes the method for involuntary hospitalization if necessary.

The court may order the hospitalization of an inmate for care or treatment if, after a hearing, the court finds by a preponderance of the evidence that the inmate is suffering from a mental disease or defect for the treatment of which he or she is in need of hospitalization. See 18 U.S.C. § 4245(d). Section 4245(e) provides that the commitment may be discharged upon certification from the Warden that the inmate has recovered to an extent that he or she is no longer in need of hospitalization, or upon the expiration of the sentence of imprisonment.

E. Title 18 U.S.C. Section 4246: Hospitalization of a Mentally Incompetent Person Due for Release

Title 18 U.S.C. § 4246 provides for the commitment and hospitalization of an inmate who is scheduled for release but who is found to be suffering from a mental disease or defect, and his or her release would create a substantial risk of bodily injury to another person, or serious damage to the property of another. If the director of a medical facility certifies that the inmate meets the standards set forth in § 4246(a), the director will file such certificate with the clerk of court. The certificate must also certify that suitable arrangements for state custody and care are unavailable. A defendant found not competent and not restorable to stand trial under § 4241(d), is also subject to the provisions of § 4246 if he or she meets the criteria for commitment. Once the certificate has been filed, the offender's release is stayed. The clerk of the court will send a copy of the certificate to the offender, to the attorney for the government, and if the person was committed under § 4241(d), to the committing court. See 18 U.S.C. § 4246(a).

The court will order a hearing to determine whether there is clear and convincing evidence the person suffers from a mental disease or defect, such that his or her release would create a substantial risk of bodily injury or serious damage to property. If sufficient evidence exists, the court will commit the person to the custody of the Attorney General. See 18 U.S.C. § 4246(d).

The Attorney General will make continuous reasonable efforts to release the person to the appropriate official of the state in which the person is domiciled or was tried. If the state refuses to assume responsibility for the offender's custody, care, and treatment, the Attorney General will hospitalize the individual for treatment in a suitable facility until the state assumes such responsibility or until the person's mental condition is such that his or her full release, or conditional release, would not pose a substantial risk of injury to other persons or damage to property. The director of the medical facility may initiate discharge proceedings in accordance with § 4246(e), or counsel for the inmate may seek discharge by filing a motion for a hearing.

A motion by counsel for the inmate seeking discharge may be filed only after 180 days from the date of a court determination that the person should continue to be committed. See 18 U.S.C. § 4247(h).

F. Title 18 U.S.C. Section 4248: Civil Commitment of a Sexually Dangerous Person

The Walsh Act, also known as the Sex Offender Registration and Notification Act (SORNA), enacted at 42 U.S.C. § 16911, provides for the civil commitment of sexually dangerous persons. Title 18 U.S.C. § 4248 provides that the BOP may institute proceedings by certifying that a person is sexually dangerous. A sexually dangerous person (SDP) is defined in §4247(a)(5) as one "who has engaged or attempted to engage in sexually violent conduct or child molestation and who is sexually dangerous to others." Pursuant to § 4247(a)(6), a person is considered sexually dangerous to others if he "suffers from a serious mental illness, abnormality, or disorder as a result of which he would have serious difficulty in refraining from sexually violent conduct or child molestation if released." The Walsh Act requires the BOP to determine if an inmate being released is sexually dangerous, and to submit certification to the district court where the person is confined, to determine if civil commitment is necessary.

The BOP Sex Offender Certification Review Branch (SOCRB) oversees the civil commitment process. SOCRB reviews the assignments of all inmates prior to release, to ascertain whether there is any history of relevant conduct. For inmates with a record of attempted or actual sexual violence or child molestation, an assessment is made of empirically-based static and dynamic risk factors. Psychological and legal records are also examined. Consideration is given to a wide range of factors including criminal history, social and family support, mental and physical health, institution conduct, and other data. The Certification Review Panel (CRP) is tasked with making the final certification determination. Should the CRP find that an individual is an SDP, certification may delay the inmate's release. A District Court judge in the federal jurisdiction in which the offender is held will conduct a hearing and determine the merits of the CRP finding. If the court concurs with the CRP determination, the inmate is placed in the custody of the Attorney General as a civil commitment, and is then held indefinitely. Efforts are then made to secure placement with the individual's state of residence. If those efforts are unsuccessful, the inmate will remain in the BOP as a resident in the Commitment and Treatment Program (CTP) until such time as the court of commitment determines the individual to be no longer sexually dangerous.

G. Title 18 U.S.C. Section 4205: *Examination of an Inmate Eligible for Parole*

This statute was repealed (along with others pertaining to parole) in 1987. However, inmates whose offenses were committed prior to November 1, 1987 ("old law") may remain parole eligible. The statute requires the BOP to furnish to the United States Parole Commission (USPC) an evaluation of an inmate's suitability for parole, including his or her mental and physical health, past criminal history, and social background.

H. Title 18 U.S.C. Sections 3552(b) and (c): *Presentence Study and Psychological or Psychiatric Examination*

During the presentence investigative process, the court may order the defendant to undergo a psychological or psychiatric examination. The court will specify the additional information it requires before determining an appropriate sentence.

This evaluation may be completed by a community consultant "unless the judge finds that there is a compelling reason for the Study to be done by the Bureau of Prisons . . . ." The statute allows for 60 days for the completion of the Study, with an extension not to exceed 60 additional days. The format of the Study report should generally follow the format used in the other statutes, specifically addressing the court's concerns.

I.   *Title 28 U.S.C. Section 2254:*
State Custody; Remedies in Federal Courts;
Title 28 U.S.C. Section 2261:
Prisoners in State Custody Subject to Capital Sentence;
Appointment of Counsel;
Requirement of Rule of Court or Statute; Procedures
for Appointment

These sections together concern state inmates who have capital sentences and who bring a writ of habeas corpus before a federal court. Mental capacity evaluations, analogous to 18 U.S.C. § 3596(c), may be ordered by the federal judge. There is no requirement that this evaluation be conducted in any particular facility. Since the inmate is serving a state sentence, it is appropriate that the evaluation be completed by a licensed or certified psychiatrist or psychologist in the state facility in which the inmate is housed.

IV.   SENTENCING ISSUES

The United States Sentencing Commission (U.S.S.C.) has published, pursuant to 28 U.S.C. §§ 991-998, the U.S. SENTENCING GUIDELINES MANUAL, to provide a general framework for sentencing. The following is a discussion of the most frequently used sanctions available in the federal criminal justice system.

A.   *Probation and Conditions of Probation*

The federal sentencing court may impose a sentence of probation with conditions placed on the offender. The offender is monitored by the U.S. Probation Office.

1.   *Community Confinement*

As a condition of probation, a defendant may be sentenced to community confinement, defined as residence in "a community corrections facility." See 18 U.S.C. § 3563 (b)(11). The BOP makes available to the courts federally-contracted Residential Reentry Centers (RRCs). An offender subject to a term of community confinement as a condition of probation or supervised release is placed in the most restrictive component of the RRC, and has limited access to the community. RRCs are available for both male and female offenders. See Program Statement 7300.09, Community Corrections Manual. The court may also place an offender in an RRC in lieu of revocation of probation or supervised release for technical violations.

2. Intermittent Confinement

Weekend terms and other forms of intermittent confinement may be imposed as a special condition of probation or supervised release. See 18 U.S.C. § 3563(b)(10). Ordinarily in these instances, the respective BOP Residential Reentry Management office will coordinate the assignment of an appropriate non-BOP detention facility, and the United States Probation Office will monitor the defendant's period(s) of intermittent confinement.

3. Home Detention

Federal sentencing guidelines (USSG 5C1.1) allow home detention as a condition of probation or a condition of supervised release as a substitute for imprisonment in certain instances. Title 18 U.S.C. § 3624(c)(2) allows for pre-release custody of an inmate in home confinement, discussed below in section K, Pre-Release Custody. Ordinarily, inmates on home detention are electronically monitored through services contracted by the Administrative Office of the United States Courts. The BOP is not involved in the post-release home detention program for probationers or supervised releases.

B. Imprisonment

The BOP maintains safe and humane correctional environments for offenders sentenced to a term of imprisonment. The appropriate United States Probation Office provides the BOP with the Presentence Investigation Report (PSR), Judgment in a Criminal Case (J&C), and Statement of Reasons (SOR) after sentencing. These documents are crucial to BOP staff decision-making to determine an inmate's facility designation, including appropriate security level, relevant programs, and subsequent pre-release preparation. The PSR and SOR contain sensitive information regarding an inmate's social contacts and criminal history, and are not permitted to be retained in the possession of the inmate. Inmates may request to review these documents, maintained in the Inmate Central File, by submitting a request for staff. See Program Statement 1351.05, Release of Information.

1. Institutional Confinement

Title 18 U.S.C. § 3621(a) authorizes the BOP to confine persons sentenced to a term of imprisonment. Institutions are classified by security level: Minimum, Low, Medium, High, and Administrative, which may house an offender of any security level. Institution security levels are determined by various factors including type of perimeter security, number of towers or external patrols, detection devices, security of housing areas, type of living quarters, and level of staffing.

2. Service of Sentence in Non-Federal Facilities

The BOP will often contract with a local jail or detention center to house an inmate sentenced to a term of one year or less, and long-term offenders may also be housed under contract with state correctional systems, or in a privately-run facility. An inmate may be transferred to a state facility or to a privately-run facility for a number of reasons, for example, should the individual present special management problems, require protection, or if his or her notoriety precludes incarceration in any BOP facility.

3. Juvenile Offenders

Federal adjudication of juveniles is governed by the Juvenile Justice and Delinquency Prevention Act (JJDPA), codified at 18 U.S.C. §§ 5031-5042. See also Program Statement 5216.05, Juvenile Delinquents. JJDPA addresses the adjudication of an offender who has not reached his or her 18th birthday, and generally prohibits housing juveniles with adult offenders. Given the very small number of federally-sentenced juveniles, operation of a separate BOP facility for this population is not practical. Therefore, the BOP contracts for placement of these offenders in state and local facilities, some of which are operated by private firms.

The JJDPA addresses three categories of inmates. The BOP's treatment of each group differs as follows:

Confinement of Persons Under Age 18 - Any inmate who has not attained the age of 18 at the time of commitment will be placed in a non-federal juvenile facility. See 18 U.S.C. § 5039.   Generally, the BOP attempts to place such inmates in community-based juvenile facilities located in or near their home communities.

Confinement of Persons 18 to 21 Years of Age - An inmate who is sentenced as an adult pursuant to 18 U.S.C. § 5032 shall be designated to an adult institution according to BOP designation criteria. An inmate who is sentenced as a juvenile will be treated as a person under 18 years of age, unless he or she has a concurrent federal adult sentence of a length equal to or greater than the juvenile sentence. If there is a concurrent federal sentence equal to or greater in length than the juvenile sentence, the inmate will be housed in an adult facility. The court imposing the juvenile sentence will be notified of this fact. If an inmate sentenced as a juvenile also has a consecutive adult sentence, he or she will be treated as a person under the age of 18 until the expiration of the juvenile sentence, or in some instances, until he or she has reached the age of 21.

Persons Who Turn 21 While Serving a JJDPA Sentence - A person who had been adjudicated as delinquent may then be designated to a BOP institution as an adult, once he or she reaches the age of 21. However, a change in placement is not required, and the BOP may retain the inmate in a contract juvenile facility for continuity of program participation.

C. Judgment in a Criminal Case (J&C)

The BOP is charged with interpreting and administering the provisions of the Judgment in a Criminal Case (formerly, Judgment and Commitment Order, or J&C) of the federal courts, as follows.

1. Judicial Recommendations for a Specific Institution, Geographic Area, or Specialized Program

The BOP has sole authority to designate the place of confinement for federal prisoners. See 18 U.S.C. § 3621(b). By statute, the BOP is required to consider the resources of the facility, the nature and circumstances of the offense, the history and characteristics of the prisoner, recommendations of the court, and guidance issued by the USSC. Initial designation decisions and decisions to transfer prisoners from one facility to another are ultimately the responsibility of the BOP and are made in accordance with Program Statement 5100.08, Inmate Security Designation and Custody Classification. The J&C may indicate the sentencing court's recommendation to house the inmate in a specific institution, geographic area, or specialized program. While every effort is made to comply with the court's recommendation, conflict with BOP policy and sound correctional management may prevent honoring the court's recommendation.

Prior to finalizing plea agreements or other concessions affecting a defendant's conditions of confinement, the parties involved should consult with the relevant CLC office regarding factors that might affect availability of the program, or the eligibility of an individual defendant for any program assignment. Specific programs or institution placements should not be part of any agreement or promised to any criminal defendant. This is particularly important when defendants carry both state and federal sentences, as complex issues arise over which sovereign has priority to implement its sentence.

2. Sentence Calculation

The BOP's Designation and Sentence Computation Center (DSCC), in Grand Prairie, Texas, oversees both initial designations and redesignations of inmates, and all sentence computations. The BOP is solely responsible for calculating federal terms of imprisonment. See United States v. Wilson, 503 U.S. 329 (1992). BOP policies and instructions to staff for the calculation of terms of imprisonment includes Program Statements 5880.28, Sentence Computation Manual (CCCA of 1984); 5880.30, Sentence Computation Manual ("Old Law"-Pre-CCCA-1984); 5880.33, District of Columbia Sentence Computation Manual; and 5110.16, Administration of Sentence for Military Inmates. Specific questions related to sentence calculation should be directed to the DSCC, telephone (972) 352-4400; e-mail at GRA-DSC/PolicyCorrespondence&AdminRemedies.

A prisoner challenging the calculation of a particular sentence does so by filing a Petition for Writ of Habeas Corpus, pursuant to 28 U.S.C. § 2241, in the U.S. District Court possessing personal jurisdiction over his or her immediate custodian (Warden). However, inmates are required to exhaust the administrative remedy process within the BOP prior to seeking judicial relief. See Program Statement 1330.17, Administrative Remedy Program. We request the court contact us if questions arise as to how a J&C will be interpreted, so that potential problems may be avoided. Occasionally, a J&C may direct the defendant's term of imprisonment to be calculated in a manner contrary to law. The BOP will then notify the prosecuting Assistant U.S. Attorney and/or the Court to resolve the conflict.

3. Commencement of a Term of Imprisonment

Title 18 U.S.C. § 3585(a) dictates that "[a] sentence to a term of imprisonment commences on the date the defendant is received in custody awaiting transportation to, or arrives voluntarily to commence service of sentence at, the official detention facility at which the sentence is to be served." Consequently, J&Cs directing a defendant's term of imprisonment to commence at a date earlier than its date of imposition, or some other date, are viewed by the BOP as contrary to statute, and notice will be given to the Court.

4. Credit for Prior Custody ("Jail Time")

Title 18 U.S.C. § 3585(b) dictates the method of calculating credit for prior custody of defendants whose offense was committed on or after November 1, 1987. Sentence credit is awarded for any time spent in official detention prior to the date a term of imprisonment commences, provided it was served as a result of the offense for which the sentence was imposed, or as a result of any offense (state or federal) for which the defendant was arrested after committing the offense for which the federal sentence was imposed. Additionally, the time must not have been credited against any other sentence. Slightly different rules apply for defendants whose date of offense is prior to November 1, 1987. See 18 U.S.C. § 3568 (repealed).

After a defendant is sentenced, the BOP is responsible for determining what period(s) of prior custody may be credited toward the federal term of imprisonment. See United States v. Wilson, 503 U.S. 329 (1992). Periods spent on pretrial release, no matter how restrictive, cannot be awarded as prior custody credit to U.S. Code offenders. See Reno v. Koray, 515 U.S. 50 (1995). D.C. Code felony offenders, however, may be entitled to such credit. See Program Statement 5880.33, District of Columbia Sentence Computation Manual. Consequently, J&Cs must be carefully drafted to avoid requiring prior custody credit awards in circumstances which are contrary to statute. In those infrequent instances in which a sentence being imposed is "adjusted," for a period of time already served, the court should note on the J&C the amount of time by which the sentence is being adjusted, the undischarged term of imprisonment for which the adjustment is being given, and that the sentence imposed is a sentence reduction pursuant to U.S.S.G. § 5G1.3(b), for a period of imprisonment that will not be credited by the BOP. See U.S.S.G. § 5G1.3, Imposition of a Sentence on a Defendant Subject to an Undischarged Term of Imprisonment, App. Note 2(C), Imposition of Sentence. Otherwise, it may appear that prior custody credit is being awarded contrary to 18 U.S.C. § 3585(b).

5. Credit for Satisfactory Behavior ("Good Conduct Time")

Title 18 U.S.C. § 3624(b) provides Good Conduct Time (GCT) credit for U.S. Code felony offenders whose offense was committed on or after November 1, 1987, and D.C. Code felony offenders whose offense was committed on or after August 5, 2000. Under that provision, inmates serving sentences greater than one year, but less than life, may receive up to 54 days sentence credit per year served. Inmates sanctioned for violating prison disciplinary rules may lose all or part of these credits. See Program Statement 5270.09, Inmate Discipline Program.

In light of the specific sentence credit applications involved, sentencing courts must be very specific in wording the J&C. For example, defendants sentenced to a "one year" term of imprisonment will actually serve one year, without the benefit of any GCT credit. Defendants sentenced to "a year and a day" term of imprisonment, however, can receive credit for satisfactory behavior and thus can actually serve less than one year. The DSCC should be consulted to provide assistance in wording the J&C, to effect the Court's intention in accordance with applicable statutes and BOP policy.

For inmates whose offense was committed on or after November 1, 1987, § 3624(b) allows 54 days of credit "at the end of each year of the prisoner's term of imprisonment." Barber v. Thomas, 560 U.S. ___ , 130 S. Ct. 2499 (2010). This does not mean that inmates serve only 311 days for every year of imprisonment imposed. Rather, inmates serve 365 out of 419 days (365 + 54 = 419) of the sentence.   For example, consider the case of an inmate sentenced to a three-year term of imprisonment on January 1, 1992.   On January 1, 1993, the inmate receives 54 days good conduct time, leaving 676 days remaining in his or her sentence (2 years minus 54 days).   On January 1, 1994, the inmate receives another 54 days of GCT, leaving 257 days remaining in his or her sentence (1 year minus 108 days). The inmate will not earn another 54 days of GCT against his or her sentence after January 1, 1994, as he or she does not have 365 days remaining to serve. Instead, the final award of GCT will be prorated for the final 257 days, resulting in an award of 33 days. The total deduction against the sentence in this case is 141 days (54+54+33), not 162 (54+54+54). The Bureau's interpretation and application of its method of calculating 54 days sentence credit was upheld by the United States Supreme Court in Barber v. Thomas. Sentence credit for satisfactory behavior by U.S. Code offenders whose offense was committed prior to November 1, 1987, is governed by Title 18 U.S.C. §§ 4161- 4166 (repealed).   Until 1987, such defendants were eligible to accrue both Statutory Good Time (§ 4161) and Extra Good Time (§ 4162). Statutory Good Time may be forfeited in whole or in part if the prisoner violates institution rules or commits any offense. See 18 U.S.C. § 4165.

6. *Fines and Costs of Confinement*

Pursuant to U.S.S.G. § 5E1.2, the court shall impose a fine in all cases, unless the defendant lacks the necessary financial resources to make payments.   For offenses committed on or after November 1, 1987, the court cannot require that any fine imposed be paid as a precondition for release from imprisonment. This is a change from prior law, which permitted the court to order the defendant to remain in prison until the fine is paid, unless and until a determination was made that the defendant was indigent or otherwise unable to pay the fine. See Program Statement 5882.03, Fines and Costs for Old Law Inmates.   The Court Security Improvement Act of 2007, Pub. L. No. 110-117, amended Title 18 U.S.C. § 3624(e), by striking the provision that prohibited releasing an inmate to supervised release unless the inmate agreed to adhere to an installment schedule to pay for any court-ordered fine imposed for the current offense.   The statute requires only that the BOP notify the inmate upon release of the releasee's requirement to adhere to the court-ordered payment schedule.

The Application Notes to the Sentencing Guidelines refer the court to the BOP and the Administrative Office of the U.S. Courts for assistance in determining an appropriate fine to cover the costs of confinement. Should the court wish, the BOP will furnish the court with the average cost of confinement at all facilities, as an inmate may be held in several different facilities during a single term of imprisonment. For prisoners for whom the court did not assess a fine to cover the costs of incarceration, and for whom the court did not waive the fine due to indigence, the BOP is authorized to collect a fee equal to the cost of one year of imprisonment, or a prorated amount, if the defendant is sentenced to a shorter term. See 18 U.S.C. § 4001 (note) and Program Statement 5380.06, Cost of Incarceration Fee (COIF). The yearly average cost of incarceration for a federal inmate in a BOP facility for Fiscal Year 2013 was $29,291.25; in an RRC, that cost was $26,612.15.

The BOP is authorized to require inmates transferred to RRCs to pay a portion or all of the costs of their confinement, and with few exceptions, all employed offenders confined in RRCs must make payments toward their housing costs. See 18 U.S.C. § 3622(c)(2). Funds collected are not returned to the BOP, but are paid to the United States Treasury. Nevertheless, requiring such payments is an effective means for the government to recover some of the costs of operating the criminal justice system, and may encourage offenders to become responsible members of the community.

7. *Inmate Financial Responsibility Program*

To assist in the collection of court-ordered financial obligations, the BOP operates the Inmate Financial Responsibility Program (IFRP) in conjunction with the Administrative Office of the U.S. Courts. See Program Statement 5380.08, Financial Responsibility Program, Inmate. All inmates with financial obligations including special assessments, restitution, fines and court costs, state or local court obligations, and other federal obligations, are encouraged to work with staff to develop an individual financial plan.

Participation in IFRP, while voluntary, is tied to eligibility for prison privileges including preferred housing, job assignments, and community activities such as community confinement and furloughs. Participation is also tied to institutional program and custody level changes. If eligible for parole, the inmate's progress in meeting his or her financial plan is a factor considered at the parole hearing. Inmates are responsible for making all payments from funds in their inmate accounts, including funds from outside resources and pay from work in the institution, or a combination of the two.

All sentenced inmates are required to work in an institutional job assignment or UNICOR work assignment with the exception of those who are unable to work for security, educational, or medical reasons. See Program Statement 5251.06, Inmate Work and Performance Pay. Inmates may also earn bonus pay for outstanding work performance. An inmate with a Court-ordered financial obligation is given preference for assignment to UNICOR, and such an assignment requires that 50% of the inmate's earnings are applied to payment of that obligation.

The sentencing court can require inmates to pay fines and special assessments as part of the judgment. If the court either orders that these financial obligations are "due immediately," or if the J&C is silent as to when they are due, then the BOP will collect those fines and special assessments through the IFRP. In the latter case, 18 U.S.C. § 3572(d) requires "immediate" payment.

15

If the sentencing court orders a defendant to pay restitution under the Mandatory Victim Restitution Act of 2006 (MVRA), Pub. L. 113-65, codified at 18 U.S.C. § 3663A, as part of the judgment, most circuits have also held that the court must also set out a schedule of payments for that restitution. One circuit has held that the BOP may not use the IFRP to collect payments toward an MVRA restitution order, unless the order also includes such a schedule. As a result, if the sentencing court intends that the defendant make payments toward restitution while imprisoned, then the J&C should contain specific language, such as "while serving the sentence of imprisonment, the defendant must make payments toward the restitution obligation at the rate of no less than $25.00 per quarter."

Regardless of the type of financial obligation ordered in the J&C, the court should avoid ambiguous language such as "payments as directed by BOP." Such statements are ordinarily construed as an improper delegation of judicial authority and could result in the exclusion of the restitution award from the amounts collected by the BOP under the IFRP.   The J&C should either specify that the financial obligation is "due immediately," or the J&C should remain silent as to when due.   Wording such as "payments to be made as directed by BOP staff" or "payments to be made in installments as set by the IFRP" is ambiguous and may result in the defendant's non-participation in the IFRP. The CLC attorney should be consulted to provide assistance in properly wording the J&C to reflect the court's intention.

V. POST-CONVICTION ISSUES

A. Designation to a Facility for Service of a Term of Imprisonment

1. Security Designation and Custody Classification

Following the imposition of a sentence of imprisonment, the BOP begins the process of designating the defendant to a facility for service of the sentence.   Title 18 U.S.C. § 3621 authorizes the BOP to designate where a prisoner will serve his or her sentence.   The BOP retains exclusive discretion to assign or to transfer any prisoner to any facility.   See Classification of Inmates, 28 C.F.R. pt. 524, subpt. B, and Program Statement 5100.08, Inmate Security Designation and Custody Classification.

The DSCC is responsible for initial custody classification, designation, assignment of BOP management variables and public safety factors, and all sentence calculation. The DSCC is not, however, responsible for assignment to, or transfer of, inmates from their designated institution to an RRC for § 3624(c) pre-release purposes.   Subsequent to the inmate's designation to an institution, institution staff members are responsible for the security and custody classification of the inmate.   The DSCC first receives notification of a newly-sentenced federal offender from the U.S. Marshal in the sentencing district.   If the court does not direct the defendant to self-surrender, the USMS will arrange for transportation of the inmate to the designated institution. See Program Statement 5100.08, Inmate Security Designation and Custody Classification.

Designation decisions take into account a number of factors including the level of security and

16

staff supervision the inmate requires, and the level of security and staff supervision the institution provides. Other considerations include matching the medical care needs of an inmate with the level of care provided by the institution, as well as the inmate's program needs (e.g., substance abuse treatment, education and vocational training, individual and/or group counseling, medical/ mental health treatment). Various administrative factors will affect the designation, including institution current bed space capacity, proximity to the inmate home location, judicial recommendations, separation needs, and security measures required to ensure the safety of victims, witnesses, and the general public.

2. DNA Collection

In accordance with 42 U.S.C. § 14135(a)(1)(A)(5), 28 C.F.R. pt. 28, subpt. B, and Program Statement 5311.01, Inmate DNA Sample Collection Procedures, the BOP collects DNA (deoxyribonucleic acid) samples from all federal inmates, usually obtained through buccal collection. DNA samples collected from individuals or derived from crime scene evidence are analyzed to produce DNA profiles that are entered in the FBI Combined DNA Index System. DNA profiles assist in identifying offenders; excluding innocent persons; solving past and future crimes; and combating recidivism through inclusion in the database. Inmates who refuse to provide a DNA sample are counseled regarding their lawful obligation and the consequences of non-compliance, which may include progressive administrative sanctions and criminal prosecution.

3. Transportation to a Designated Institution

After an initial designation has been made, an inmate may be transported to the assigned facility by the USMS, either by vehicle or contract carrier airline. The USMS also operates a fleet of aircraft in conjunction with the Justice Prisoner and Alien Transportation System (JPATS). Additionally, BOP ground transportation and support provide for economical and expeditious movement of inmates.

On occasion, the court may order a defendant to voluntarily surrender at the facility to which he or she is initially designated. The BOP draws a positive inference from the court's determination that the defendant is sufficiently trustworthy to surrender voluntarily, and self-surrender will favorably impact the inmate in terms of classification and designation decisions.

4. Interstate Agreement on Detainers

Many prisoners in BOP custody have detainers for unresolved criminal charges pending against them in one or more jurisdictions. To facilitate programming designed for treatment and rehabilitation, and to resolve pending matters, BOP joins with many states as a party to the Interstate Agreement on Detainers (IAD). See Program Statement 5800.15, Correctional Systems Manual. This agreement enables a jurisdiction carrying an untried criminal indictment, information, or complaint, to secure temporary custody of the inmate. Such proceedings may be initiated by the state or by the inmate. Program Statement 5800.15 delineates the appropriate procedures for a jurisdiction to obtain custody of an inmate with a detainer lodged by a member state. <u>See</u> Program Statement 5875.12, <u>Transfer of Inmates to State Agents for Production on State Writs</u>.

5. *Central Inmate Monitoring System*

The BOP monitors and controls the transfer, temporary release on writ, and community activities of certain inmates who present special management needs or security concerns. <u>See</u> <u>Central Inmate Monitoring System</u>, 28 C.F.R. pt. 524, subpt. F; Program Statement 5180.05, <u>Central Inmate Monitoring System</u>. Central Inmate Monitoring (CIM) inmates require a higher level of review which may include Central Office and/or Regional Office clearance for transfers, temporary releases, or community activities. Monitoring does not preclude a CIM inmate from such activities when the inmate is otherwise eligible, but contributes to the safe and orderly operation of federal institutions and to the protection of the public.

Special measures are taken to protect at-risk inmates. CIM inmates may include, among others, persons whose incarceration generates public notoriety; individuals who have cooperated with law enforcement authorities; inmates who have made threats against government officials, and inmates identified as gang members. While in custody, an offender may require separation from other inmates stemming from such events that either preceded confinement, or occurred during incarceration. Accordingly, procedures such as a separation assignment have been developed to ensure the safety of such individuals. If deemed necessary, such a classification may continue throughout the period of incarceration.

6. *Communication Management Units*

The BOP operates two Communication Management Units (CMUs), located at FCI Terre Haute, Indiana, and at USP Marion, Illinois. CMUs were established in 2006 and 2008, respectively, to house inmates who, due to their current offense of conviction, offense conduct, or other verified information, require increased monitoring of communications between the inmate and persons in the community to protect the safety, security, and orderly operation of the BOP and to protect the public. Inmates designated to the CMU may have been convicted of, or associated with, terrorism or terrorist organization, repetitively attempted to contact their victims; and/or attempted illegal activities through approved communication methods and/or received extensive disciplinary action due to misuse of approved communicating methods.

The CMU is a general population unit, with access to customary inmate activities, such as recreation, religious services, and education programming. All communications, however, are subject to increased monitoring. All incoming and outgoing general correspondence is reviewed by staff prior to delivery to the inmate or delivered for mailing through the U. S. Postal Service. Telephone communication and social visits are limited, live-monitored by staff; and must occur in only in English unless conducted through simultaneous translation monitoring.

7. Special Management Units

This initiative, as detailed in Program Statement 5217.01, <u>Special Management Units</u>, was implemented to enhance the agency's ability to manage some of the most disruptive and problematic inmates in the BOP. The Special Management Units (SMUs) provide a controlled and restrictive environment for inmates who exhibit behavior that is violent, confrontational, can extremely disruptive to the orderly running of the institution. Inmates participating in disruptive behavior, gang activity, introduction of drugs, weapons, and cell phones may be referred to an SMU. SMU designation is non-punitive, and while conditions of confinement are more restrictive than for general population inmates, the inmate may earn increased privileges by progressing through the four-level SMU program, at which time they are eligible for redesignation to the general population.

B. Admission and Orientation Program for Inmates

Every inmate designated to a BOP institution is required to participate in the Admission and Orientation (A&O) program. <u>See</u> Program Statement 5290.14, <u>Admission and Orientation Program</u>. Staff presentations provide each inmate with written materials describing institution operations, program availability, inmate rights and responsibilities, and the BOP inmate discipline process. Each inmate receives an introduction to all aspects of the institution and meets with staff from the case management, medical, and mental health units.

C. Programs and General Services

Research has demonstrated that inmate participation in programs teaching marketable skills helps to reduce recidivism rates. Additionally, institution misconduct can be significantly reduced through programs emphasizing personal responsibility, respect, and tolerance of others. Accordingly, the BOP offers inmates program opportunities to adopt positive social values and life skills. Programs include working in prison industries and other job assignments, vocational training, mock job fairs, drug treatment, faith-based residential programs, parenting skills, and other activities described in greater detail below.

1. Education and Recreation Programs

The BOP is committed to providing inmates, within a secure environment, with opportunities to gain skills needed for successful reentry to the community. Program Statement 5300.21, <u>Education, Training, and Leisure Time Program Standards</u>, requires each institution to maintain an Education Department responsible for providing inmates with literacy classes and other related educational programs. Every institution provides both leisure and law library services. <u>See</u> Program Statement 1542.06, <u>Library Services, Inmate</u>, and Program Statement 1315.07, <u>Legal Activities, Inmate</u>.

Title 18 U.S.C. § 3624(f) mandates an education program for those federal prisoners who are not functionally literate. Non-English speaking inmates are required to participate in an English-as-a-

Second Language program until able to function in the English language at the eighth grade level, pursuant to 18 U.S.C. § 3624(f)(4). With few exceptions, inmates lacking either a high school diploma, or a General Educational Development credential (GED), are required to enroll in an adult literacy program for a minimum of 240 hours. See 28 C.F.R. pt. 544, subpt. H. Should an inmate prematurely end his or her participation prior to program completion, the inmate will lose some Good Conduct Time if governed by that statutory provision. Upon completion of the 240 hour course, an inmate may choose to end participation in adult literacy classes. However, to encourage the inmate to participate in such programs until earning the GED, incentive awards are available. Work pay and Good Conduct Time potential are limited for inmates who choose to discontinue program participation without obtaining a GED.

The Violent Crime Control and Law Enforcement Act of 1994 (VCCLEA), Pub. L. No. 103-322, enacted on September 13, 1994, mandates that an inmate with a date of offense on or after September 13, 1994, but not before April 26, 1996, lacking a high school diploma or GED credential, must participate and make satisfactory progress in the literacy program in order to vest earned Good Conduct Time. The Prison Litigation Reform Act of 1995, (PLRA), Pub. L. No. 104-134, enacted April 26, 1996, provides that in determining Good Conduct Time awards, the BOP shall consider whether an inmate with a date of offense on or after April 26, 1996, who lacks a high school diploma or GED, participates in and makes satisfactory progress in the literacy program, in order to be eligible to earn the maximum amount of Good Conduct Time. A foreign national, who is subject to a final confirmed order of removal, deportation, or exclusion, is exempt from the satisfactory progress requirement of the literacy program provisions of VCCLEA and PLRA. See 28 C.F.R. pt. 523, subpt. C.

BOP programming emphasizes reentry skills, offering a variety of programs for self-improvement, including occupational training, resume writing, job fairs, and parenting skills. Recreation programs encourage inmates to make constructive use of leisure time, with both group and individual activities. Physical fitness and wellness programs, such as nutrition and weight control, are provided during non-working hours to promote positive lifestyle changes. See 28 C.F.R. pt. 544, subpt. D, and pt. 553, subpt. B, and Program Statement 5370.11, Recreation Programs, Inmate. Hobby craft programs vary from institution to institution, and may include painting, leather crafts, artwork, and ceramics. Completed projects are mailed home, as inmates are not permitted to retain completed projects in their possession.

2. Religious Programs

Title 28 C.F.R. pt. 548, subpt. A, Religious Programs and Program Statement 5360.09, Religious Beliefs and Practices set forth BOP policy for inmates who wish to practice their religion while incarcerated. Each institution is assigned a staff Chaplain, who both ministers to the inmate population, and serves as a department head to arrange for contract religious clergy and volunteers from the community to assist in group worship, individual religious counseling, spiritual guidance, and the study of sacred writings. Group worship is conducted when security conditions permit. All institutions provide an opportunity for individual worship.

3. Food Service

BOP offers nutritionally balanced, appetizing meals. Special Food and Meals, 28 C.F.R. pt. 547, subpt. C and Program Statement 4700.06, Food Service Manual, provide that medical diets be available to inmates who require such diets. All inmates, except those on medical or religious diets, are served the same meals in a dining room setting when consistent with the security and orderly operation of the institution. Staff dining rooms serve the same meals offered to inmates. In addition, inmates with religious dietary requirements may apply for the religious diet program, designed to address the dietary restrictions of a variety of different faith groups. Meatless food options are offered as a component of the religious diet program. See Program Statement 5360.09, Religious Beliefs and Practices.

The BOP follows a standardized menu. The National Menu is designed not only to bring consistency to BOP Food Service operations, but also to ensure Heart Healthy options are available to increase the ability to prevent and manage chronic health issues of our inmate population. Heart Healthy options, with lower fat and sodium levels, are available and the Warden at any institution may choose to serve only the Heart Healthy food options at select meals. High security institutions may modify the National Menu to address security concerns.

4. Work Programs and UNICOR

All federal inmates are required to work with the exception of those who for security, educational, or medical reasons are unable to do so. See Inmate Work and Performance Pay Program, 28 C.F.R. pt. 545, subpt. C; Program Statement 5251.06, Inmate Work and Performance Pay. An institution work day is ordinarily seven hours. Most inmates are assigned to an institution job such as food service worker, orderly, plumber, painter, warehouse worker, or groundskeeper, earning 12 cents to 40 cents per hour.

Inmates may apply for an assignment to Federal Prison Industries (FPI). FPI, under the trade name UNICOR, employs over 13,000 inmates. In accordance with statutory mandates, UNICOR (1) provides employment and industrial skills training to as many inmates as possible; (2) produces market-priced, quality goods for federal government customers; (3) operates in a self-sustaining manner; and (4) minimizes its impact on private business and labor. See 18 U.S.C. § 4122. UNICOR job wages currently range from $0.23 cents to $1.15 per hour. Inmates may also earn bonus pay for outstanding work performance. See Program Statements 8120.02, Work Programs for Inmates, FPI; 8000.01, UNICOR Corporate Policy and Procedures.

UNICOR is a wholly-owned federal government corporation and does not receive Congressional appropriations for its operations. See 18 U.S.C. § 4122(b)(1) and Program Statements 8000.01, UNICOR Corporate Policy and Procedures; 8120.02, Work Programs for Inmates, FPI. Title 18 U.S.C. § 4121 et seq., when read together with Title 10 U.S.C. § 2410n and Section 637 of the Consolidated Spending Bill for FY 2005 (Division H), Pub.L. No. 108-447, require federal departments, agencies, and government institutions to purchase products listed on UNICOR's schedule of products from UNICOR, when those products are comparable to products offered by private vendors in terms of price, quality, and time of delivery. If UNICOR's products are not comparable, then the federal purchaser may procure the product through a competitive solicitation, provided that UNICOR is given an opportunity to compete. UNICOR also provides a variety of services on a competitive basis.

5. *Inmate Accident Compensation*

Inmates are not federal employees and are not subject to the Fair Labor Standards Act or other federal employee compensation laws. If an inmate is injured while performing an assigned duty, he or she must immediately report the injury to the work supervisor. The work supervisor will secure medical treatment for the inmate and file an injury report with the institution safety manager. See Program Statement 1600.09, Occupational Safety, Environmental Compliance, and Fire Protection. Pursuant to 18 U.S.C. § 4126, and Inmate Accident Compensation, 28 C.F.R. pt. 301, inmates may be compensated for injuries caused by the actual performance of their work assignments in UNICOR or in other institution work assignments. The Inmate Accident Compensation program is the exclusive remedy available to inmates who sustain work-related injuries and is the exclusive remedy for subsequent medical care of work-related injuries. Inmates may not recover damages in tort for work-related injuries. See Federal Tort Claims Act, 28 U.S.C. § 2671, et seq.; United States v. Demko, 385 U.S. 149 (1966).

(a) Lost-Time Wage Program

Inmates injured in the course of performing their work assignments, and who are medically excused for at least three consecutively scheduled work days, may receive lost-time wages equal to 75 % of the standard hourly rate for their regular work assignments. Pursuant to 28 C.F.R. pt. 301 subpt. B, an Institution Safety Committee oversees the Lost-Time Wage Program. A lost-time wage payment continues until the inmate is released, transferred to another institution (for reasons unrelated to the injury), returns to the work assignment, or refuses to return to work. An inmate dissatisfied with any decision regarding lost-time wages may appeal the decision pursuant to Program Statement 1330.17, Administrative Remedy Program.

(b) Compensation for Work-Related Physical Impairment or Death

No more than 45 days prior to the date of an inmate's release, but no less than 15 days prior to this date, an inmate who feels that a residual physical impairment exists as a result of a prison work-related injury may apply for compensation. Should circumstances not permit such a submission, a claim may be accepted up to 60 days following release or up to one year after release, for good cause shown. This program is administered from the Central Office, and any questions may be directed to the Claims Examiner, Inmate Accident Coordinator. A claim for compensation as the result of a work-related death may be filed by a dependent of the deceased inmate up to one year after the inmate's work-related death. See 28 C.F.R. pt. 301, subpt. C.

6. *Female Offenders*

Female inmates are not housed with male inmates. At various sites, female offender units are co-located with male units. However, all housing units and activities are separate. Appropriate programs and services are provided to meet the physical, social, and psychological needs of female offenders. Programming is in parity with that offered to male inmates, tailored to be gender-responsive. See Program Statement 5200.01, Female Offenders, Management of.

The designation and classification system for female offenders acknowledges empirical evidence that female offenders are less likely to be violent or attempt escape. Bed space for female offenders is available at varied security levels.

(a) Birth Control and Pregnancy

The BOP provides female inmates with medical and social services related to pregnancy, birth control, child placement, and abortion. See 28 C.F.R. pt. 551, subpt. C, and Program Statement 6070.05, Birth Control, Pregnancy, Child Placement and Abortion. Each female offender having child bearing potential is medically screened for pregnancy upon admission, and is instructed to inform medical staff should she suspect she may be pregnant, so that pre-natal care may be immediately provided.   Childbirth typically takes place at a community hospital.   While placement of the child in the community is the inmate's responsibility, staff will assist the inmate and work closely with community agencies to effect an appropriate arrangement.

The BOP offers a community residential program for pregnant inmates, Mothers and Infants Together (MINT). The MINT program, managed by private social service agencies under contract to the BOP, provides mothers with childbirth, parenting, and coping skills classes. In addition to parenting services, MINT sites offer chemical dependency treatment, physical and sexual abuse counseling, self-esteem building programs, budgeting classes, and vocational and educational programs. It is at the discretion of the inmate's institution housing Unit Team to decide whether to refer the inmate to MINT. A MINT participant may remain at the residential program for a period after birth, to provide an opportunity to bond with her newborn child before returning to an institution to complete her sentence. Prior to the birth, the mother must make arrangements for an appropriate custodian for the child. An inmate is eligible to enter the program if she satisfies the general criteria for furlough eligibility, and is in her final two months of pregnancy.   See Program Statement 5280.09, Inmate Furloughs. Designation to the MINT program is in accordance with Program Statement 7310.04, Community Corrections Center (CCC) Utilization and Transfer Procedures.

(b) Abortion

In Roe v. Wade, 410 U.S. 113 (1973), the Supreme Court decided that a woman has a fundamental right of privacy to choose to terminate her pregnancy. The Court has also made clear, however, that the exercise of such a choice need not be carried out through the use of federal funds.   See Rust v. Sullivan, 500 U.S. 173 (1991).

Pursuant to 28 C.F.R. pt. 551, subpt. C, and Program Statement 6070.05, Birth Control, Pregnancy, Child Placement, & Abortion, the Warden provides each pregnant inmate with medical, religious, and social counseling to aid her in making the decision whether to carry the pregnancy to term or to have an elective abortion. The BOP will assume all costs associated with the abortion procedure only when the life of the mother would be endangered if the fetus is carried to term, or in the case of rape. In all other cases non-BOP funds must be obtained to pay for any abortion procedure. Whether or not the BOP pays for the abortion, the BOP may expend funds to escort the inmate to a facility outside the institution to receive the procedure.

7. *Substance Abuse Treatment*

Drug abuse education and substance abuse treatment is available in each institution. See Program Statement 5330.11, Psychology Treatment Programs. Inmates identified with a history of drug use, a judicial recommendation for treatment, a violation of supervision related to drug use, or an instant offense related to drug use, are required to take the BOP's drug abuse education course. Inmates who are found to have a drug use problem are also referred for nonresidential drug abuse treatment.

At the end of FY 2013, the BOP had residential drug abuse programs (RDAP) at 81 facilities, including one for Spanish-speaking male inmates, and one for Spanish-speaking female inmates, to address the needs of inmates with a diagnosis of substance abuse or dependence based on the American Psychiatric Association Diagnostic and Statistical Manual of Mental Disorders. Dual Diagnosis RDAP programs have been developed to address the needs of inmates with a co-existing substance abuse and mental health diagnosis. RDAP participation includes a program incentive of early release of up to one year sentence reduction for an eligible inmate's sentence in accordance with VCCLEA, 18 U.S.C. § 3621 (e) (2). Successful completion of RDAP requires the participant to receive no less than 120 days of community-based treatment by licensed providers during his or her residence in an RRC or on home detention. To receive the program incentive, the inmate must successfully complete RDAP and must also satisfy the eligibility requirements provided in 28 C.F.R. pt. 550, subpt. F, and Program Statement 5331.02, Early Release Procedures under 18 U.S.C. § 3621(e). In all cases, however, the award of a sentence reduction is at the discretion of the BOP.

The BOP's drug abuse treatment strategy parallels community drug abuse treatment regimens differentiating between residential treatment (RDAP) and out-patient treatment (non-residential treatment). This approach allows the BOP to provide the intensity of treatment appropriate for the needs of inmates with a history of substance abuse.

.

8. *Urine Surveillance Program*

Illegal drug use compromises institutional security and threatens inmate and staff safety, and the BOP maintains careful oversight to detect and deter inmate drug use. See Program Statement 6060.08, Urine Surveillance and Narcotic Identification. Urine screening is a very effective tool in detecting drug use in the institution. Inmates involved in community activities are routinely tested for the use of illegal drugs, and inmates are tested based on individualized suspicion of drug use. In addition, a random sample of the total inmate population at each institution is tested monthly. Any inmate testing positive for unauthorized substances, or who refuses to submit to such a test, is subject to sanction, including the loss of early release earned through successful RDAP completion.

Any visitor or staff member found to be introducing illegal drugs or other contraband into an institution is immediately subject to arrest. See 18 U.S.C. §§ 1791, 3571, 28 C.F.R. pt. 511, and Program Statement 5510.15, Searching, Detaining, or Arresting Visitors to Bureau Grounds and Facilities. By entering or attempting to enter BOP grounds or facilities, the individual has consented to search of his person and his belongings. A visitor who refuses to comply with authorized search procedures will be denied entry or be required to leave.

9. Medical Services

(a) Medical Services Available to Sentenced Offenders

Every institution maintains a Health Services Unit to provide medical, dental, and mental health care. BOP policy regarding medical care and procedures for caring for inmates with medical needs is set forth in Medical Services, 28 C.F.R. pt. 549, and Program Statement 6031.03, Patient Care. Service is provided by a variety of health care professionals, including psychiatrists, physicians, nurses, physician assistants, dieticians, dentists, and pharmacists. BOP health care staff is augmented by assigned United States Public Health Service personnel. Community medical professionals are consulted as needed, and inmates are sent to community hospitals should medically necessary care be unavailable at the institution. See Program Statement 6010.02, Health Services Administration.

In making determinations regarding the appropriate institution in which to house an offender, the BOP carefully considers the offender's health status. As the BOP provides extensive medical services, a defendant's medical condition generally will not preclude a sentence to BOP custody. When serious health concerns are an issue in a designation decision, the DSCC will refer the case to the BOP's Office of Medical Designations and Transportation (OMDT). A specific institution is designated with attention to the urgency of medical need; institution capability; current bed space availability; and security concerns. BOP facilities are classified by the intensity level of health care resources.

Each inmate is assigned a medical "Care Level," based on his or her medical history as described in the Presentence Report and other available information. The BOP's goal in implementing the Care Level system is to assign inmates with greater medical needs to those facilities with more comprehensive on-site medical resources, and to provide more effective and efficient access to health care for each inmate.

Inmates with Care Level 1 needs are generally healthy, under 70 years of age, and may have limited medical needs requiring clinician evaluation and monitoring. Examples of such conditions are mild asthma, diet-controlled diabetes, and patients with human immunodeficiency virus (HIV) who are stable and do not require medications.

Inmates with Care Level 2 needs are those who are stable outpatients, requiring at least quarterly clinician evaluation. Examples of such conditions are medication-controlled diabetes, epilepsy, and emphysema.

Inmates with Care Level 3 needs are fragile outpatients who require frequent clinical contacts, and/or who may require some assistance with activities of daily living, but do not require daily nursing supervision. This Care Level may include stabilization of medical or mental health conditions that may require periodic hospitalization. Other examples of this Care Level are patients with cancer in remission less than a year, advanced HIV disease, severe mental illness in remission on medication, severe congestive heart failure, and end-stage liver disease.

Inmates with Care Level 4 needs are severely impaired, and may require daily nursing care. Examples of such conditions are those with cancer in active treatment, dialysis, quadriplegia, stroke or head injury patients, major surgical patients, acute psychiatric illness requiring inpatient treatment, and high-risk pregnancy.

The DSCC designates those inmates with Care Levels 1 and 2. For those inmates with Care Levels 3 and 4, the designation decision will be made by the OMDT, as the medical need of the inmate is the primary factor in the designation decision.

(b) Medical Referral Centers

Medical, dental, and mental health services at each institution are provided according to the Care Level. Six federal medical referral centers (FMCs) provide specialized health services:

FMC Butner, North Carolina

Located north of Raleigh, FMC Butner is part of the Federal Correctional Complex (FCC) and serves as a major medical and psychiatric referral center for male inmates. FMC Butner has all specialty areas of medicine and is the primary referral center for oncology, providing chemotherapy and radiation therapy. FMC Butner manages a broad range of subacute and chronically ill inmates and an orthopedic surgery program is available. Dialysis services are provided on-site.

FMC Carswell, Fort Worth, Texas

Located in Fort Worth in the northeast corner of the Naval Air Station, Joint Reserve Base, FMC Carswell serves as the major medical and psychiatric referral center for female inmates. All specialty areas of medicine are available at FMC Carswell, through in-house staff and community-based consultant specialists.

FMC Devens, Massachusetts

Located in central Massachusetts, northeast of Worcester, FMC Devens serves both medical and mental health care needs of male inmates. All specialty areas of medicine are available at FMC Devens, through in-house staff and community-based consultant specialists. Additional services provided at FMC Devens include dialysis treatment for inmates with end-stage renal failure.

FMC Lexington, Kentucky

Located just north of Lexington, FMC Lexington treats male inmates. All specialty areas of medicine are available at FMC Lexington, by in-house staff and community-based consultant specialists. FMC Lexington serves as the primary referral center for inmates with most types of leukemia and lymphoma. Outpatient forensic studies may be performed at FMC Lexington.

FMC Rochester, Minnesota

Located 80 miles southeast of Minneapolis, FMC Rochester serves as a major medical and mental health referral center for male inmates. Most specialty and sub-specialty consultations are available through the Mayo Clinic, and in other local facilities. FMC Rochester is the primary referral center for inmates with end-stage liver disease and advanced HIV infection, as well as other infectious diseases requiring long-term management. FMC Rochester provides extensive psychiatric and psychology services, including inpatient psychiatry services and forensic studies. Outpatient forensic studies are not performed at FMC Rochester.

U.S. Medical Center for Federal Prisoners (USMCFP), Springfield, Missouri

Located in southwest Missouri, USMCFP Springfield is a major medical and psychiatric referral center for male inmates. All specialty areas of medicine are available at USMCFP Springfield, through in-house staff and community-based consultant specialists. Springfield is the primary referral center for high security inmates. The institution maintains extensive psychiatric and psychological services, to include inpatient forensic studies. It is the major kidney dialysis center for the BOP.

(c)   Voluntary Mental Health and Medical Treatment

In accordance with Program Statements 6031.03, Patient Care; 6340.04, Psychiatric Services; and 5310.12, Psychology Services Manual, the health care mission of the BOP is to provide appropriate and necessary medical, dental, and mental health services to inmates by professional staff. As in the community, each individual inmate is responsible for self-care, and for seeking medical services when necessary. Regardless of Care Level, each inmate is assigned to a Primary Care Provider Team designed to function in the same manner as a community medical team practice. Whenever possible, the inmate will see the same medical provider(s) for each appointment, ensuring continuity of care and economy of service.

Patient care is provided by appointment, scheduled in advance through request by the inmate, or scheduled by the provider for follow-up examination. A nominal co-pay for inmate-initiated medical visits is assessed to encourage responsible use of health care resources, but no inmate is denied care because of inability to pay.   See Program Statement 6031.02, Inmate Copayment Program. Prescribed medications are given free of charge, in accordance with an established National Formulary. Certain over-the-counter medications may be purchased in the inmate commissary. <u>See</u> Program Statement 6541.02, <u>Over-the-Counter Medications</u>. Generally, inmates may keep prescribed medications within their possession. Controlled medication is individually dispensed by medical staff.

(d) Managing Infectious Disease

Inmate education plays a large role in the BOP's effort to prevent and manage infectious disease. Inmates are provided information on a continuing basis to address disease prevention, both within the institution and in preparation for release. The BOP has adopted a multi-faceted program of testing, treatment, and education, and the rate of HIV (human immunodeficiency virus), tuberculosis (TB), and other infectious diseases in the inmate population does not significantly differ from that in the community. All sentenced inmates are tested for HIV on initial admission, when clinically indicated, and on request of the inmate at the discretion of staff. They are also tested for purposes of infectious disease monitoring, and at the request of the inmate. While inmates with HIV are housed in the general population, HIV-positive inmates who demonstrate predatory or promiscuous behavior may be isolated in order to protect other inmates from becoming infected. The BOP also maintains an active program to control and treat contagious TB. Each inmate is required to undergo TB screening within two calendar days of initial incarceration. Inmates who are free from prior TB infection are screened annually for newly-acquired TB infection, and when clinical staff determines that the inmate may be at risk for infection. <u>See</u> <u>Procedures for Handling of HIV Positive Inmates Who Pose a Danger to Others</u>, 28 C.F.R. pt. 541, subpt. E, and Program Statement 6190.03, <u>Infectious Disease Management</u>.

10. Mental Health Counseling and Treatment Services

Inmates are offered a full range of mental health services, through staff psychologists and psychiatrists, as well as through community mental health specialists. <u>See</u> Program Statements 5310.12, <u>Psychology Services Manual</u>; 6010.02, <u>Health Services Administration</u>; 6340.04, <u>Psychiatric Services;</u> 5310.13, <u>Mentally Ill Inmates, Institution Management of</u>; and 6010.03, <u>Psychiatric Evaluation and Treatment</u>.   Many inmates can be treated on an outpatient basis. Inmates requiring in-patient treatment are referred to one of several psychiatric referral centers: FMC Rochester; USMCFP Springfield; FMC Butner; FMC Devens; and FMC Carswell for female inmates. Psychiatric medication is used only for a diagnosed psychiatric disorder for which such medication is the most appropriate treatment. <u>See</u> 28 C.F.R. pt. 549, subpt. C; Program Statement 6010.03, <u>Psychiatric Evaluation and Treatment</u>.   Psychiatric treatment is available on-site, through telemedicine evaluation, or by community consultants.

Suicide prevention is a major concern at all institutions.   Program Statement 5324.08, <u>Suicide Prevention Program</u>, emphasizes staff training to alert staff to signs of those inmates who may be contemplating suicide, and provides for comprehensive prevention programs.

(a) Involuntary Mental Health Treatment

The Supreme Court has held that the Due Process Clause permits prison officials to involuntarily medicate a mentally ill inmate with psychotropic medication if the inmate is dangerous to self, either actively or by being gravely disabled, or to others, and if such treatment is in the prisoner's medical interest. See Washington v. Harper, 494 U.S. 210 (1990). See also United States v. Sell, 539 U.S. 166 (2003) (holding that if medication is to be involuntarily administered solely for the purpose of restoring an inmate's competency, the decision must be made by the trial court); 28 C.F.R. pt. 549, Administrative Safeguards for Psychiatric Treatment and Medication, and Program Statement 6010.03. Such treatment is permissible after the inmate has received notice and a hearing before an administrative panel.[3] In a psychiatric emergency, psychotropic medication may be administered involuntarily, if the medication is an appropriate treatment for the mental illness, and other alternatives would not be effective. Inmates given emergency treatment of this type will be considered for referral to a BOP psychiatric referral center.

(b) Mental Health Programs

Psychology staff is available at all institutions to provide inmates with counseling and other mental health services. Staff facilitate ongoing counseling programs, conduct personal crisis intervention, and are readily accessible to inmates as needed. Staff or contract psychiatrists are available for individual consultation.

All inmates are screened by Psychology Services staff during the institution's Admission and Orientation Program. Screening may include an individual interview. Psychologists are available for individual and group counseling, and inmates interested in these services may submit a request for participation to a staff member in Psychology Services. Mental health services are offered to treat drug use and alcohol abuse, as well as other behavioral and emotional problems. See Program Statement 5310.12, Psychology Services Manual. In addition, BOP staff in each housing unit are available for informal counseling sessions and conduct formal group counseling activities through Alcoholics Anonymous, anger management, and other groups. Inmate participation in these activities is voluntary, and encouraged.

(c) Sex Offender Management and Treatment

The BOP maintains a comprehensive sex offender management strategy, implemented to effectively manage its population of sex offenders, and manage the risks posed by these offenders to the general public. With the passage of the Walsh Act, as codified in 18 U.S.C. § 3621(f), Sex Offender Management, the BOP has further expanded its monitoring, evaluation, and treatment programs for sex offenders.   Inmates with a history of sexual offenses may be designated to the Sex Offender Management Program (SOMP), at one of eight institutions. A residential program is located at FMC Devens. Non-residential programs are located at FCI Elkton, FCI Englewood, USP Marion, FCI Marianna, FCI Petersburg, FCI Seagoville, USP Tucson, and at FMC Carswell for female inmates. Assignment is made in accordance with the security level of the individual.

---

[3]Medication may be administered without an administrative hearing for emergencies in which a person is suffering from a mental illness which creates an immediate threat of bodily harm to self or others, serious destruction of property, or extreme deterioration of functioning secondary to psychiatric illness. See 28 C.F.R. pt.549, subpt. C.

An inmate amenable to treatment is offered participation in the Sex Offender Treatment Program, non-residential (SOTP-NR), offered at all SOMP institutions. The SOTP-NR is designed to meet the treatment needs of low and moderate risk sexual offenders. SOTP-NR offers inmates individualized non-residential treatment, ordinarily involving six to eight hours of programming per week, over a nine-month period.

Male inmates at any BOP institution may volunteer for an intensive residential sex offender treatment program (SOTP-R), offered at FMC Devens. Placement in the SOTP-R is reserved for high risk sexual offenders, based on the extent and seriousness of the inmate's offending history. The SOTP-R is a therapeutic community, housed in a 112-bed specialized unit. The program employs a wide range of cognitive-behavioral therapies to help the sex offender manage his sexual deviance both within the institution and in preparation for release. Ordinarily, participants complete the program in 12 to 18 months.

BOP informs tribal, state, and local law enforcement agencies of the release of a sex offender, and notifies the released inmate of his or her legal obligation to register with local authorities, as required by the Sex Offender Registration and Notification Act (SORNA), enacted as part of the Walsh Act. The BOP assists the released sex offender with information regarding community treatment programs available to them upon release from federal custody. See 18 U.S.C. § 4042(c), and Program Statement 5141.02, Sex Offender Notification and Registration.

(d) Implementation of the Prison Rape Elimination Act of 2003

The Prison Rape Elimination Act of 2003 (PREA), Pub. L. No. 108-79, was enacted by Congress to address sexual abuse of offenders to include all public and private institutions housing adults and juveniles, as well as in community-based facilities. Pursuant to 28 C.F.R. pt. 115, and Program Statement 5324.11, Sexually Abusive Behavior Prevention and Intervention Program, the BOP maintains a zero tolerance approach to prison rape. The BOP has implemented PREA by prevention planning; training and education of staff, volunteer, contractors, and inmates; screening for risk of sexual victimization and abusiveness; and insuring that any incident is reported, investigated, and that perpetrators are effectively disciplined. Inmates are encouraged to report sexual abuse to a staff member, and to inform staff if the inmate has witnessed sexually abusive behavior. BOP staff keep reported information confidential, discussing the case with officials only on a need-to-know basis, and only for law enforcement or investigative purposes.

Should an inmate not feel comfortable talking with staff, inmates are instructed to use special mail procedures and write directly to the Warden, Regional Director, or Director. An inmate may send an e-mail directly to the Office of the Inspector General of the Department of Justice if he or she wishes to do so. Every allegation is investigated and staff take appropriate steps to both safeguard inmates and to prosecute perpetrators.

(e) Treatment of Inmates with Gender Dysphoria

Part of the implementation of PREA is increased sensitivity to the needs of the transgendered or intersex inmate. An inmate with a possible diagnosis of Gender Dysphoria (GD), will receive thorough medical and mental health evaluations from medical professionals. An inmate will not be physically examined for the sole purpose of determining the inmate's genital status. See 28 C.F.R. pt. 115(3) and Program Statement 5324.11. If an inmate's genital status is unknown, staff may review medical records, converse with the inmate, or if necessary, be ascertained as part of a broader medical examination. Program Statement 6031.03, Patient Care, provides that the inmate with a diagnosis of GD will receive a proposed treatment plan to promote the physical and mental stability of the patient. The treatment plan may include elements or services that were, or were not, provided prior to incarceration. Treatment plans will be reviewed regularly and updated as necessary. Each treatment plan or denial of treatment will be reviewed by the BOP Medical Director of the BOP Chief Psychiatrist, and hormone therapy may be a consideration. Inmates will receive a current individualized assessment and evaluation. No treatment option is precluded solely due to the level of services that an inmate received, or did not receive, prior to incarceration.

D. *Visiting, Telephones, and Correspondence*

1. *Visiting*

Inmates are encouraged, throughout their incarceration, to maintain ties with their family and friends in the community. Inmates are ordinarily permitted face-to-face visitation with approved family and friends in the institutions' general visiting room area. Attorney visits are afforded as much privacy as possible to ensure confidentiality. See Program Statement 5267.08, Visiting Regulations. Conjugal visits are not permitted. Each institution schedules its own visiting hours and procedures. Inmates receive this information during the admission and orientation (A&O) process, so they can advise family members and others of the visiting requirements. Visitors should also consult the BOP website for individual institution visiting instructions and scheduled hours. Pretrial inmates may receive visits in accordance with the local institution's guidelines for visiting. However, staff may allow a pretrial inmate special visits to protect the inmate's business interests, or to help prepare for trial. See 28 C.F.R. pt., subpt. J, and Program Statement 7331.04, Pretrial Inmates.

Inmates have no constitutional right to social prison visits, and the courts have accorded substantial deference to the judgment of prison administrators to place limitations on inmate visiting. Based on security concerns, institutions may restrict visitation. An inmate's visiting privileges may be withheld as a disciplinary sanction.

2. *Telephones*

Telephone privileges are another means of maintaining community and family ties. See Telephone Regulations for Inmates, 28 C.F.R. pt. 540, subpt. I, and Program Statement 5264.08, Inmate Telephone Regulations. Inmates may call friends and family outside the institution on a telephone provided for that purpose. An inmate's telephone time is ordinarily limited to 300 minutes per calendar month. Limitations and conditions may be imposed upon an inmate's telephone privileges to ensure consistency with other aspects of correctional management responsibilities.

Inmates are advised of the institution's telephone monitoring capability, and a notice is posted at each inmate telephone advising that calls are monitored. Use of the telephone constitutes consent to the monitoring of calls. Ordinarily, calls are paid for by the inmate, but in some cases the receiving party pays. See 28 C.F.R. pt. 540, subpt. J. Unmonitored calls to attorneys are permitted in limited circumstances. See Section F, Inmate Access to Court, Unmonitored Legal Telephone Calls, infra. Third-party or other alternative call arrangements are not permitted, thus limiting the opportunity for inmates to use the phones for criminal or other inappropriate purposes. Inmates are not permitted possession or use of cellphones or electronic communication devices. Any such possession or use is grounds for disciplinary action and possible criminal prosecution.

3. Written and Electronic Correspondence

Inmates are encouraged to write to family, friends, and other community contacts during incarceration. See 28 C.F.R. pt. 540, subpt. B, and Program Statement 5265.14, Correspondence. Inmate correspondence is classified as either "general" or "special" mail. "General mail" is opened and inspected by staff for both contraband and content which might threaten the security or good order of the institution. Incoming "special mail" is opened only in the presence of the inmate, and inspected for physical contraband and the qualification of any enclosures as special mail. Consult Program Statement 5265.14 for detailed discussion of "general" and "special" mail procedures. Inmates are not permitted use of express mail services.

All BOP facilities provide eligible inmates with the capability to send and receive electronic messages using dedicated BOP computers. See Program Statement 5265.13, Trust Fund Limited Inmate Computer System (TRULINCS)-Electronic Messaging. TRULINCS is funded entirely by the Inmate Trust Fund, which is maintained by profits from inmate purchases of commissary products and telephone services, and the fees inmates are pay for using TRULINCS. Inmates have no access to the Internet. As with traditional mail communication, all such messages are subject to staff monitoring, including an inmate's electronic communication with his or her attorney. Message content is subject to the same restrictions as regular mail.

Inmates (other than pre-trial detainees), may not direct a business while incarcerated. This does not, however, prohibit correspondence necessary to enable an inmate to protect property and funds that were legitimately the inmate's at the time of commitment. For example, an inmate may correspond about refinancing an existing mortgage or sign insurance papers, but may not operate a mortgage or insurance business while in the institution.

Inmates are permitted to receive commercial publications from the community. See 28 C.F.R. pt. 540, subpt. F, and Program Statement 5266.11, Incoming Publications. Inmates are permitted to subscribe to, or receive by mail, publications without prior approval. The BOP has established procedures to determine if an incoming publication is detrimental to the security, discipline, or good order of the institution, might facilitate criminal activity, or is otherwise prohibited by law, and will reject publications which are found to meet that criteria.

E. Inmate Discipline Procedure

Pursuant to 18 U.S.C. § 4042(a)(3), the BOP administers an inmate disciplinary process to promote a safe and orderly environment for inmates and staff. After arriving at a BOP facility, all inmates receive written notice of their rights and responsibilities, prohibited acts within the institution, the possible range of sanctions for each offense, and disciplinary procedure.

Violation of a prohibited act carries sanctions corresponding to the severity of the offense. Sanctions may include time in disciplinary segregation, loss of good time credits, and loss of privileges. See 28 C.F.R. pt. 541, subpt. A, and Program Statement 5270.09, Inmate Discipline Program. Only institution staff may take disciplinary action against inmates. Corporal punishment, as well as retaliatory and capricious disciplinary action, is not permitted under any circumstance.

Consistent with the minimum procedural protections required by Wolff v. McDonnell, 418 U.S. 539 (1974), the BOP disciplinary process requires that staff provide the inmate with a written copy of the charges, and that the inmate is entitled to be present during the initial hearing. An inmate is not permitted a staff representative nor to call witnesses at a Unit Discipline Committee (UDC) hearing, but may present documentary evidence. However, at a Discipline Hearing Officer (DHO) hearing, the inmate may request a staff representative and may have witnesses appear at the proceeding. An attorney may not represent the inmate at either hearing. Inmates may appeal the decision of the UDC or the DHO through the Administrative Remedy program. See 28 C.F.R. pt. 542, subpt. B, and Program Statement 1330.17, Administrative Remedy Program.

F.   *Inmate Access to Court*

The BOP affords an inmate reasonable access to legal materials and to his or her attorney, and reasonable opportunity to prepare legal documents. See 28 C.F.R. pt. 543, and Program Statement 1315.07, Legal Activities, Inmate.

1. *Law Libraries*

All federal prisons maintain electronic inmate law libraries. Legal materials maintained in the inmate law libraries include federal court decisions, federal statutes, and a number of other publications, as noted in Program Statement 1315.07. Inmates not physically able to utilize the main law library (inmates in segregation status, or those with a medical disability), are assisted by staff to access law library resources. In many cases, legal resource materials may be available to inmates during evening and weekend hours. Inmates with pending court deadlines may be given additional time to use the law library. An inmate may solicit or purchase legal materials from outside the institution, pursuant to Program Statement 5266.11, Incoming Publications.

2. *Preparation of Legal Documents*

Inmates are permitted a reasonable amount of time, ordinarily when not participating in a scheduled program or work assignment, to conduct their own legal research and to prepare legal documents. See 28 C.F.R. pt. 543, subpt. B, and Program Statement 1315.07. Inmates ordinarily have access to photocopying machines, typewriters, and office supplies. For safety, security, and fire hazard reasons, inmates are limited in the amount of legal materials they may possess. See Program Statements1315.07, and 5580.08, Inmate Personal Property. Inmates may generally assist each other in preparing legal documents, absent unique security concerns. However, one inmate may not possess another inmate's legal materials except when assisting another inmate in the institution's main law library or in another location designated by the Warden. Any assistance offered by one inmate to another is voluntary. An inmate is not entitled to assistance from any specific inmate, and no inmate may receive compensation for assisting another.

3. *Attorneys*

At every institution inmates are permitted to contact and retain attorneys. See Retention of Attorneys, 28 C.F.R. pt. 543, subpt. B, and Program Statement 1315.07, Legal Activities, Inmate; Program Statement 7331.04, Pretrial Inmates; and 28 C.F.R. pt. 551, subpt. J, Pretrial Inmates, Access to Legal Resources. Attorney visiting takes place during regular institution visiting hours. Attorney visits for pretrial inmates may be conducted at times other than established visiting hours with the approval of the Warden or designee. Attorneys and, in some cases, their representatives, may generally visit inmate clients in private conference rooms if available, or in other accommodations designed to ensure a reasonable degree of privacy. Attorney representatives, such as interpreters, paralegals, and private investigators, must contact the institution's legal department in advance in order to complete the necessary documentation to be permitted to visit and inmate on behalf of an attorney. Legal visits are visually monitored, as necessary, but are not subject to auditory monitoring. See, 28 C.F.R. pt. 543, subpt. B, Visits by Attorneys.

4. *Legal Mail*

Particular care is taken to ensure that "special mail" (mail to or from courts, attorneys, and certain government officials) is kept confidential. See 28 C.F.R. pt. 540, subpt D, Special Mail, and Program Statement 5265.14, Correspondence. Special mail from attorneys must be marked "Special Mail-Open only in the presence of the inmate." In addition, the sender must identify himself or herself on the envelope as a person entitled to invoke the protections of special mail. The sender's return address must reference an individual identified as an attorney, not a firm, e.g., "John Doe, Attorney," not "Law Offices of Smith & Smith." Incoming special mail is opened in the presence of the inmate and is visually inspected for contraband. Staff may inspect incoming special mail to determine that it qualifies as such, but may not otherwise review its content.

To reduce the likelihood that inmates will successfully send harmful materials to persons in the community by exploiting the privacy afforded outgoing special mail, all outgoing special mail from an inmate must be delivered directly to a staff member for further processing. Staff then confirm that the inmate delivering the outgoing special mail to be sent out is the same inmate reflected in the return address. Inmates may seal outgoing special mail, before submitting directly to staff for further processing. All outgoing special mail is subject to scanning by electronic means.

5. *Unmonitored Legal Telephone Calls*

Inmates may place unmonitored telephone calls to their attorneys. See 28 C.F.R. § 540.102 and

Program Statement 5264.08, Inmate Telephone Regulations. To do so, inmates must specifically request staff assistance to first approve the call, and then place the call on an unmonitored staff telephone. A pretrial inmate may telephone his or her attorney as often as resources of the institution allow. See, 28 C.F.R. pt. 551, subpt. J, Access to Legal Resources and Program Statement 7331.04, Pretrial Inmates. To receive permission to place an unmonitored attorney call, an inmate is ordinarily required to establish that his or her communication with attorneys by other means is not adequate. The 300-minute per calendar month limitation does not apply to unmonitored legal telephone calls. Inmate requests for unmonitored attorney calls are carefully reviewed. Frequent unmonitored telephone calls increase an inmate's opportunity to pursue illegal activities without detection, and require an inordinate amount of staff time.

6. Inmate Involvement in Litigation While Incarcerated

(a) Depositions

Should an attorney wish to take an inmate's deposition, the attorney must contact the inmate directly. If the inmate wishes to cooperate, the attorney should then contact the relevant CLC covering the institution in which the deposition is to be held, to assist in making arrangements. Video or tape recorders are not permitted inside the institution without the prior written permission of the Warden. Such requests must be processed and approved prior to scheduling a visit. Visiting regulations apply, and all equipment is subject to search. Leave of a court of competent jurisdiction must be obtained prior to taking any deposition of a federal inmate. See FED. R. CIV. P. 30(a)(2). At the discretion of the Warden, a room may be made available for the deposition, should the inmate consent to be deposed.

(b) Subpoenas

Response to a subpoena by BOP staff will be processed in accordance with applicable policy. See, 28 C.F.R. pt. 513, Release of Information and Program Statement 1351.05, Release of Information. Should an attorney request the appearance of a staff member in a court proceeding, or request the production of documents by subpoena, the CLC attorneys will consult with the relevant U.S. Attorney's Office, in accordance with 28 C.F.R. pt. 16, subpt. B, Production or Disclosure in Federal or State Proceedings. Frequently, a request for documents may be more efficiently handled through a Freedom of Information Act (FOIA) request, rather than by subpoena. Consult the relevant CLC for additional information.

(c) Inmate Civil Suits – Service of Process

The BOP will not accept service of process for an inmate. Anyone desiring to serve an inmate may use a local process server, or otherwise follow local court procedures in the jurisdiction in which the inmate is housed. Wardens may require local process servers effectuating in-person service to be a law enforcement officer acting in that capacity, or to undergo a criminal background check. The prospective process server is advised to contact the CLC with responsibility for the institution in which the inmate is housed, for specific information.

(d) Court Appearance of an Inmate

In accordance with 28 C.F.R. pt. 527, subpt. D, and Program Statement 5875.12, <u>Transfer of Inmates to State Agents for Production on State Writs</u>, the BOP will consider the request of a state or local court for the transfer of an inmate to local physical custody pursuant to a state writ of habeas corpus *ad prosequendam* or *ad testificandum)*. Such transfer is at the discretion of the Warden.   Transfers in civil cases pursuant to a writ *ad testificandum* must be cleared through both the CLC counsel and the Warden. Transfers will be recommended only if the case is substantial, where testimony cannot be obtained through alternative means such as depositions or interrogatories, and where security concerns do not preclude such a transfer.

(e) Inmate Access to Discovery Materials

In some circumstances, an inmate may access litigation documents in various electronic formats other than printed form. Electronic legal materials for inmate review should be provided on a storage device appropriate with maintaining the safety and security of the institution. Should a request be received to view legal materials in a format which is not compatible with the configuration available at the institution, staff will advise the requestor. Specific requests should be directed to the Warden of the institution in which the inmate is confined.

G. Administrative Remedy Program

The Administrative Remedy Program provides every inmate with the opportunity to seek formal review of a grievance concerning virtually any aspect of his or her confinement, should informal procedures not achieve resolution. <u>See</u>, 28 C.F.R. pt. 542, subpt. B, and Program Statement 1330.17, <u>Administrative Remedy Program</u>. This program applies to all inmates confined in institutions operated by the BOP, inmates designated to contract RRCs, and to former inmates for issues which arose during confinement. Inmates are obligated to attempt informal resolution of grievances prior to filing a formal request for administrative remedy. Once a formal request is filed at the institution level ("BP-9"), the Warden of that facility has 20 days to investigate and provide the inmate a written response. If the inmate is dissatisfied with the Warden's response, he or she has 20 days to file a Regional Administrative Remedy Appeal ("BP-10"). Once received in the Regional Office, the Regional Director has 30 days to investigate and provide the inmate a written response. If the inmate is dissatisfied with the Regional Director's response, he or she has 30 days to file a Central Office Administrative Remedy Appeal ("BP-11"). Once received in the Central Office, the Administrator, National Inmate Appeals, has 40 days to investigate and provide the inmate a written response. After receiving the Administrator's response, the inmate has exhausted the BOP's Administrative Remedy Program. The program provides for expedited investigations and responses in emergency situations, as well as providing extensions of time for both filing grievances and receiving responses. No time limit is imposed upon an inmate raising allegations of sexual abuse through the administrative remedy system.

If the inmate considers the issue to be sensitive, e.g., the inmate's safety or well-being would be placed in danger if the request became known at the institution, the inmate may submit the appeal directly to the appropriate Regional Director. The inmate must mark the request as "sensitive" and explain in writing the reason for not submitting the request at the institution. If the Regional Administrative Remedy Coordinator agrees that the request is sensitive, the request shall be accepted, investigated, and a response will be generated. Otherwise, the request will not be accepted, and the inmate shall be advised in writing of that determination, without a return of the request. The inmate may then pursue the matter by submitting a request for Administrative Remedy locally to the Warden. The Warden shall allow a reasonable extension of time for such a resubmission.

The PLRA requires prisoners to exhaust administrative remedies before filing suit in federal court. That statute provides that "[n]o action shall be brought with respect to prison conditions under section 1983 of this title, or any other Federal law, by a prisoner confined in any jail, prison, or other correctional facility until such administrative remedies as are available are exhausted." See 42 U.S.C. § 1997e(a). See also, Porter v. Nussle, 534 U.S. 516 (2002) and Booth v. Churner, 532 U.S. 731 (2001). Exhaustion is mandatory in Bivens actions. However, exhaustion in habeas petitions has been judicially created. Exhaustion should be encouraged; however, courts may waive it in cases where they believe exhaustion would have been futile. The requirement to exhaust the administrative remedy process serves to: (1) promote administrative efficiency by preventing premature judicial interference with agency processes (2) encourage respect for executive autonomy by allowing an agency opportunity to correct its own errors, (3) facilitate judicial review by affording courts the benefits of an agency's experience and expertise, and (4) serve judicial economy by having the agency compile the factual record.

The Supreme Court has reaffirmed these holdings in Woodford v. Ngo, 548 U.S. 81, 90-91 (2006), and mandated ". . .compliance with an agency's deadlines and other critical procedural rules because no adjudicative system can function effectively without imposing some orderly structure on the course of its proceedings. . . The text of 42 U.S.C.A. § 1997e(a) strongly suggests that PLRA uses the term 'exhaustion' to mean. . .proper exhaustion." Section 1997e(a) refers to 'such administrative remedies as are available' and thus points to the doctrine of exhaustion in administrative law." See also, Jones v. Bock, 549 U.S. 199 (2007).

The Administrative Remedy Program is administered differently for inmates in private facilities. Should an inmate at a private facility wish to appeal a local decision, the inmate may file with the local institution. Inmates in private facilities who wish to grieve a specific BOP matter (which is limited to classification, designation, sentence computation, reduction of sentence, removal or disallowance of Good Conduct Time, or issues directly involving BOP staff) may utilize the progressive BOP administrative remedy process available to all federal inmates. The appeal must then be filed with the Chief of the BOP's Privatization Management Branch.

H. Personal Property

Inmates may possess only that property which is authorized by policy to be retained upon admission to the institution, is issued while the inmate is in custody, is purchased in the institution commissary, or is approved by staff to be mailed to, or otherwise received by an inmate. See 28

C.F.R. pt. 553, and Program Statement 5580.08, <u>Inmate Personal Property</u>.   These rules contribute to the management of inmate personal property in the institution and contribute to a safe environment for staff and inmates by reducing fire hazards, security risks, and sanitation problems. Required hygiene items are issued by the institution, and personal preference items are available for purchase in the inmate Commissary.   <u>See</u> Program Statements 4400.05, <u>Property Management Manual</u>, and 5230.05, <u>Grooming</u>. Inmates may purchase a variety of clothing, snacks, and grooming items in the inmate Commissary at scheduled times. As of April 15, 2006, no tobacco products are sold in the Commissary, and inmates are prohibited from smoking or using tobacco in any form except for religious purposes as authorized by staff in accordance with Program Statement 5360.09.

I. Inmate Liens

The Court Security Improvement Act of 2007, Pub. L. No. 110-177, added additional restrictions to the documents an inmate may possess.   Title 18 U.S.C. § 1521 establishes a criminal offense for filing, attempting to file, or conspiring to file, a false lien or encumbrance against the real or personal property of a federal judge or federal law enforcement officer.   Secondly, 18 U.S.C. § 119 establishes a criminal offense for making publicly available "restricted personal information" about a "covered individual" with the intent to threaten, intimidate, or incite a crime of violence against such persons which includes court officers, jurors, witnesses, informants, and federal law enforcement officers. Inmate mail which contains documents determined to be related to fraudulent Uniform Commercial Code (UCC) filings, redemption, and/or copyright proceedings may be rejected as outlined in PS 5265.14, <u>Correspondence</u>.   If an inmate is found to found in possession of these types of documents or information without authorization, those items will be confiscated, and the inmate will be subject to inmate discipline. In addition, materials believed to be of a criminal nature will be reviewed to determine whether the action should be referred for criminal prosecution, as noted in Program Statement 1350.01, <u>Criminal Matter Referrals</u>.

J. Special Administrative Measures

1. National Security Cases, 28 C.F.R. pt. 501.2

Upon direction of the Attorney General, the Director may authorize the Warden to implement Special Administrative Measures (SAMs) that are reasonably necessary to prevent disclosure of classified information that would pose a threat to the national security if the inmate disclosed such information. SAMs include, but are not limited to, placing an inmate in administrative detention and restricting social visits, mail privileges, phone calls, access to other inmates and to the media.

Part 501.2 authorizes the Director, upon direction of the Attorney General, to determine the period of time an initial SAM is imposed, up to one year. The Director may also extend the SAM in increments of time not to exceed one year, if the Attorney General receives certification from the intelligence community that there is a danger that the inmate will disclose classified information and that the unauthorized disclosure would pose a threat to the national security.

2. Prevention of Acts of Violence and Terrorism, 28 C.F.R. pt. 501.3

Upon direction of the Attorney General, the Director may authorize the Warden to implement SAMs that are reasonably necessary to protect persons against the risk of death or serious bodily injury. These procedures may be implemented when there is a substantial risk that an inmate's communications or contacts with persons could result in death or serious bodily injury to persons, or substantial damage to property that would entail the risk of death or serious bodily injury to persons. Initial imposition of the SAM may be for a period of time not to exceed one year.

The Director may extend the SAM in increments of time not to exceed one year, on receipt of written notification from the Attorney General that certification was received by the Attorney General from law enforcement or the intelligence community that there continues to be a substantial risk that the inmate's communications or contacts with other persons could result in death or serious bodily injury to persons, or substantial damage to property that would entail the risk of death or serious bodily injury to persons.

K. Family Emergencies and Temporary Releases

In limited circumstances, temporary release from the prison facility may be obtained through an approved furlough or an escorted trip. See 28 C.F.R. pt. 570, subpt. C, and subpt. D; and Program Statements 5280.09, Inmate Furloughs, and 5538.05, Escorted Trips. Several factors are reviewed in determining whether a trip is permissible and how such a trip will be accomplished including the reason for the trip and the offender's criminal history, security designation, and custody classification.

1. Furloughs

A furlough is an authorized absence from an institution by a sentenced inmate without an escort from the BOP, the USMS, or other federal or state agent. See Program Statement 5280.09. For federal inmates whose offense occurred on or after November 1, 1987, 18 U.S.C. § 3622 vests the BOP with the sole authority to grant furloughs. For offenses committed prior to November 1, 1987, 18 U.S.C. § 4082 provides the authority for furloughs. The BOP has delegated this function to the Warden of the federal prison in which the inmate is incarcerated. See 28 C.F.R. § 570.32(a).

Furloughs are a privilege intended to help inmates develop release plans; re-establish family ties; participate in educational, religious, or social activities; or receive essential medical treatment that is not available in BOP custody. Except where the purpose of the furlough is to obtain necessary health care treatment, or to transfer to another facility, the inmate or the inmate's family must bear all expenses of the furlough, including transportation. Only inmates within two years of their anticipated release dates and who have community custody are eligible for non-emergency day furloughs. An inmate who meets these and other requirements set forth in policy may apply to the Warden for a furlough. Pretrial inmates are excluded from consideration. The Warden ordinarily may not grant a furlough to an inmate convicted of a serious crime against a person or whose presence in the community could attract undue public attention, or undermine the seriousness of the offense. An inmate may appeal denial of a furlough application through the Administrative Remedy Program.

2. Escorted Trips

The BOP provides approved inmates with staff-escorted trips into the community for such purposes as receiving medical treatment not otherwise available at the institution, visiting a critically ill member of the inmate's immediate family, attending a funeral, or participating in a community program or work-related function. See Program Statement 5538.05, Escorted Trips. Escorted trips fall into one of two categories, medical and non-medical. The need for an escorted trip may arise unexpectedly (e.g., to visit a critically ill family member) or may be planned in advance (e.g., to attend an educational function). In many instances, the inmate and/or family must bear the cost of an escorted trip. An inmate may appeal denial of an escorted trip application through the Administrative Remedy Program.

L. Release

1. Early Release from Prison

(a) Executive Clemency

The United States Constitution, Article II, Sec. 2, gives the President authority to issue pardons, commute sentences, remit fines, and grant reprieves to any person convicted of a federal crime. The U.S. Pardon Attorney ordinarily reviews all petitions for Executive Clemency, undertakes the necessary investigation, and prepares a recommendation for the President.

To expedite the Pardon Attorney's consideration of an inmate's petition for commutation of a sentence of imprisonment, a federal inmate seeking commutation must send the petition through the Warden to the Pardon Attorney. An inmate may request the appropriate forms and instructions for filing a petition for commutation of sentence from the inmate's case manager at the institution. Upon request from the Pardon Attorney, the Director will forward a recommendation on the inmate's petition. Staff may not refuse to process an inmate's petition for commutation of sentence, even when it appears that the inmate is not eligible. See, 28 C.F.R. pt. 1, Executive Clemency; 28 C.F.R. pt. 571 subpt. E, Petition for Commutation of Sentence; and Program Statement 1330.15, Commutation of Sentence, Petition for. Inmates seeking a pardon (rather than commutation of sentence) must wait at least five years after their release from confinement, or, if no confinement was imposed, five years after the date of conviction. No petition will be accepted from a person on probation, parole, or supervised release.

(b) Reduction in Sentence

Title 18 U.S.C. § 3582(c)(A)(i) authorizes the sentencing court to reduce an inmate's sentence upon motion of the Director of the BOP "if it finds that extraordinary and compelling reasons warrant such a reduction [and] that such a reduction is consistent with applicable policy statements issued by the Sentencing Commission." See 28 C.F.R. pt. 571, subpt. G, Compassionate Release (Procedures for the Implementation of 18 U.S.C. 3582(c)(1)(A) and 4205(g)); and Program Statement 5050.49, Compassionate Release/Reduction in Sentence: Procedures for Implementation of 18 U.S.C. 3582(c)(1)(A) & 4205(g). For inmates whose offense was committed prior to November 1, 1987, the BOP may file a motion with the sentencing court seeking to reduce the term of imprisonment to the time the inmate has served, thereby making him or her eligible for parole consideration. For persons who are already parole eligible, the BOP may recommend to the Parole Commission that the inmate be again reviewed for possible parole. See 18 U.S.C. § 4205(g). In any event, the actual release decision then rests with the Parole Commission, rather than with the sentencing court.

For inmates who offense was committed on or after November 1, 1987, the Director may request the U.S. Attorney's Office to file the BOP's motion for reduction in sentence (RIS). Inmates may request a RIS under a number of conditions enumerated in Program Statement 5050.49 and may be based on medical or non-medical circumstances. Medical circumstances include a request by an inmate who is terminally ill or debilitated. Non-medical circumstances may include elderly inmates; elderly inmates with medical conditions; circumstances in which there has been a death or incapacitation of the inmate's child's caregiver, or the incapacitation of an inmate's spouse or registered partner. When reviewing a RIS request, the Director will consider a number of factors enumerated in the Program Statement, including but not limited to the nature and circumstances of the inmate's offense; criminal history, release plan; length of time served; and possible risk to the community. In every case, the Director will solicit the input of identified victims and the U.S. Attorney's Office responsible for prosecuting the inmate. The Director may consult with the Office of the Deputy Attorney General as well. The Director will also consider D.C. Code inmates for RIS.

2. Parole

Many inmates sentenced to a term of imprisonment of more than one year for offenses committed before November 1, 1987, are eligible to be released on parole. See 18 U.S.C. § 4205; and 28 C.F.R., pt. 2.2. Parole, Release, Supervision and Recommitment of Prisoners, Youth Offenders, and Juvenile Delinquents. Generally, inmates must complete one-third of the term imposed or some other court-imposed minimum term before becoming eligible for parole. See Eligibility for parole; adult sentences, 28 C.F.R. § 2.2 and Program Statements 5800.15, Correctional Systems Manual; 5880.30, Sentence Computation Manual/Old Law/Pre CCCA 1984.

A federal inmate seeking parole must apply to the United States Parole Commission. At least 60 days prior to the initial parole hearing, the inmate is notified of the time and place of the hearing and of the right to review all documentation to be considered by the Parole Commission. See 28 C.F.R. § 2.11(e).

3. Pre-Release or Community Confinement in Preparation for Release

Pursuant to 18 U.S.C. § 3624(c) most inmates nearing release or parole from a federal institution will be housed at an RRC for transitional services during the final portion of their sentence. Such placement assists the offender in finding a job, locating a place to live, and re-establishing family ties.

RRCs are operated by a number of social service agencies and private companies under contract to the BOP. RRCs offer a broad spectrum of pre-release programs for community confinement of federal offenders. To oversee these services, the BOP maintains a network of Residential Reentry Management Offices in major cities throughout the country. See Program Statement 7300.09, Community Corrections Manual.

While BOP staff closely monitor RRCs, the RRC contractor is responsible for all aspects of the inmate's confinement. The RRC will assist the inmate in locating employment, medical care, social services, and in re-establishing community and family ties. Should an inmate violate any conditions of his or her residence at the facility, or has been involved in any further criminal activity, disciplinary sanctions will be imposed. An inmate may be returned to custody. All RRC disciplinary sanctions imposed against the inmate will be reviewed by BOP staff to ensure compliance with BOP policy.

Inmate program plans are individualized and tailored to the reintegration needs of the offender. During their stays, employed offenders are required to pay a subsistence charge to help defray the costs of their confinement in the RRC. See 18 U.S.C. § 3622(c).

4. *Home Confinement*

Home confinement provides an opportunity for offenders to assume increasing levels of responsibility while at the same time providing sufficient restrictions to promote community safety and convey the sanctioning value of the sentence. See Program Statement 7320.01, Home Confinement. Title 18 U.S.C. § 3621 requires the BOP to designate any penal or correctional facility as the place of a prisoner's confinement, accordingly, an inmate will not be designated to home confinement at the beginning of his or her sentence. Home confinement may be considered for an eligible inmate nearing the end of his or her sentence, and is an option for offenders who no longer require the structure of a halfway house. The offender remains at his or her residence during non-working hours, and may be monitored by telephonic or electronic signaling devices. See 18 U.S.C. § 3563(b)(19). Inmates may participate in home confinement only during the last 10% of their sentence or 6 months prior to their Good Conduct Release date, whichever is less. See 18 U.S.C. § 3624(c) and 28 C.F.R. pt. 570, subpt. B.

The BOP uses two different methods to monitor inmates on home confinement. The first requires the RRC to track the inmate's whereabouts and curfew compliance through daily telephone contacts and periodic personal contacts at the home and workplace. The inmate must also report to the RRC on a scheduled basis for counseling and program updates.

The second method involves electronic monitoring. Many RRCs utilize such electronic monitoring technology, usually involving the use of an ankle bracelet signaling a computer-driven receiving and recording device to detect an inmate's location.

M. Notification to the Community of the Release of an Offender

Title 18 U.S.C. § 4042(b) requires that the BOP notify tribal, state, and local law enforcement officials at least five calendar days prior to the release of an inmate to supervised release, probation, or parole, who has been convicted of a "drug trafficking crime" or a "crime of violence." Prisoners released under the protection of the Witness Protection Program may be exempt from this provision. This requirement applies to all inmates whose current offense of conviction, or whose criminal history as determined by staff, includes such a conviction. For those inmates confined in an RRC, such notification is made at least two weeks prior to the inmate's release. BOP staff supply the offender's name, criminal history, final release date to supervised release, probation or parole, the offender's projected address on supervised release, probation or parole, and any release conditions or restrictions on the conduct of the prisoner imposed by the sentencing court, other than the Standard Conditions of Supervision found on the J&C. See Program Statement 5110.15, Notification of Release to State and Local Law Enforcement Officials.

Title 18 U.S.C. § 4042(c) requires that notification must be made for those inmates who have been convicted of certain sexual offenses. Such notification operates both to ensure the safety of the community, and to ensure that inmates convicted of sex offenses are made aware of local treatment opportunities and registration requirements prior to their release. See Program Statement 5141.02, Sex Offender Notification and Registration. Notification is made to the chief law enforcement officer of the state, to the chief local or tribal law enforcement official, to the appropriate U.S. Probation Office, and in addition, to the sex offender registration official in the responsible for the receipt or maintenance of such information. Notification must be made at least two weeks prior to the release date. Further, staff must attach a completed Sex Offender Registration and Treatment Notification form, to document that the inmate was advised of sex offender registration requirements that may be operable in the releasing jurisdiction.

Sex offender registration and reporting requirements have been made more stringent with passage of the Walsh Act. The Walsh Act establishes standards for a nationwide sex offender registry, and provides grant money to the states upon compliance with the requirements of the act. It is the inmate's legal requirement to register upon release. Newly enacted 18 U.S.C. § 2250, Section 141 of the Walsh Act, creates federal criminal liability for failure to register.

Finally, the Victim and Witness Protection Act of 1982, the Crime Control Act of 1990, the Violent Crime Control and Law Enforcement Act of 1994, as well as the Attorney General's Guidelines for Victim and Witness Assistance, set forth procedures to meet the needs of crime victims and witnesses. BOP will respond to a request from a victim or witness who wishes to be notified regarding a specific inmate's release or release-related activities. See Program Statement 1490.06, Victim and Witness Notification Program. A victim or witness of a serious crime requesting to be notified of a specific inmate's release must make this request to the United States Attorney in the district where the prosecution occurred. Upon receiving such a request from the U.S. Attorney, BOP staff will promptly notify the victim or witness when his or her request for notification has been received. Staff will then notify the requestor of the initial designation of the inmate, and should the inmate be released to parole, to an RRC, or to the community, as well as any incidence of furlough, escape, death, and in the event that the offender is recommitted to custody after release from incarceration.

VI.   CONCLUSION

The Bureau of Prisons is committed to the safety of the community, and to the security and well-being of incarcerated offenders.   Consult the BOP website and contact the relevant BOP office should you have any further questions or concerns.

VII.   APPENDICES

Appendix A: Summary Table, Application of Title 18 U.S.C. Chapter 313
           Offenders with Mental Disease or Defect

Note: All examinations ordered pursuant to Chapter 313 are conducted in accordance with the provisions of 18 U.S.C. § 4247 (b) and (c). Specifically, 18 U.S.C. § 4247 (b) requires that the examination be conducted by a licensed or certified psychiatrist or psychologist and that the person to be examined be committed to the custody of the Attorney General for placement in a suitable facility. Unless impracticable, the examination shall be conducted in a suitable facility closest to the court.

Appendix B: Regional Counsel and Consolidated Legal Center (CLC) Offices

Appendix C: Relevant Acronyms

APPENDIX A: Summary Table

Application of Title 18 U.S.C. Chapter 313; Offenders with Mental Disease or Defect

Statutory Section	Role of the Attorney General	Role of State/Local Government or Agencies
PRETRIAL	PRETRIAL	PRETRIAL
§ 4241(a) – Motion for examination to determine defendant's competency to stand trial.	The defendant may be committed for a reasonable period (not to exceed 30 days) for examination; the court may approve a 15-day extension. The examination will be conducted at the nearest suitable facility to the criminal court, if practicable.	The court may permit a psychiatrist or psychologist in the community to conduct the examination. This is particularly appropriate if the defendant is on bond. The BOP will not cover the cost of an examination conducted in the community.
§ 4241(d) – Determination whether the defendant will attain competency.	If incompetent, the defendant shall be hospitalized for a reasonable period of time (not to exceed 4 months) for treatment to regain competency. The defendant may be committed for an additional reasonable period until either the defendant attains competency, or until charges are dropped. If at the end of the time period specified, it is determined that the defendant's mental condition has not so improved as to permit proceedings to go forward, the defendant is subject to the provisions of § 4246 and § 4248.	
§ 4242 – Motion for examination of a defendant who intends to rely on the defense of insanity.	The defendant may be committed for a reasonable period (not to exceed 45 days) for examination; the court may approve a 30-day extension. The examination will be conducted at the nearest suitable facility to the criminal court, if practicable.	The court may permit a psychiatrist or psychologist in the community to conduct the examination. This method is particularly useful if the defendant is out on bond. The BOP will not cover the cost of an examination conducted in the community.

Statutory Section	Role of the Attorney General	Role of State/Local Government or Agencies
POST-TRIAL	**POST-TRIAL**	**POST-TRIAL**
§ 4243(a) – Hospitalization of a person found not guilty only by reason of insanity.	The acquittee must be committed to a suitable facility for examination for a reasonable period not to exceed 45 days (the court may approve a 30-day extension), to determine if his or her release would create a substantial risk of bodily injury to others, or serious damage to the property of another.	The Attorney General may seek civil commitment under State law. See 18 U.S.C. § 4247(i)(B).
§ 4243(e) – Civil commitment should the court determine that releasing the acquittee would create substantial risk of bodily injury to others, or serious damage to the property of another.	The acquittee shall be committed to the custody of the Attorney General. The acquittee will remain hospitalized until the Attorney General is able to arrange for release to the State where the acquittee was domiciled (or tried) for treatment and care, or until the acquittee's condition has improved such that release would no longer pose a risk of bodily injury to others, or serious damage to the property of another. The director of the facility shall file annual reports regarding the acquittee's condition. See 18 U.S.C. § 4247(e).	The State may agree to assume responsibility for care and treatment of the acquittee; this includes assuming all financial responsibility. The director of the facility shall file annual reports with the court regarding the acquittee's condition. See 18 U.S.C. § 4247(e).
§ 4243(f) - Certification for discharge should the director of the facility determine that the acquittee may be released.	The director of the facility must file with the court a certificate stating that the acquittee has recovered such that release, conditionally or unconditionally, would no longer create a substantial risk of bodily injury to others, or serious damage to the property of another. The acquittee may not be released without court order.	The director of the facility must file with the court a certificate stating that the acquittee is ready to be released.
§ 4244(a) – Motion to determine whether the convicted person is suffering from mental disease or defect and requires treatment prior to sentencing.	The defendant may be committed for a reasonable period (not to exceed 30 days) for examination; the court may approve a 15-day extension.	The court may permit a psychiatrist or psychologist in the community to conduct the examination. The BOP will not cover the cost of an examination conducted in the community.

Statutory Section	Role of the Attorney General	Role of State/Local Government or Agencies
POST-TRIAL	**POST-TRIAL**	**POST-TRIAL**
§ 4244(d) – Civil commitment of a convicted defendant who is suffering from mental disease or defect and requires treatment prior to sentencing.	The defendant shall be committed for hospitalization in a suitable facility under a provisional sentence. The director of the facility must file annual reports regarding the defendant's condition. See 18 U.S.C. § 4247(e). When the defendant no longer suffers from a disease or defect, the director shall file a certificate with the court; the court may modify the provisional sentence.	
§ 4245(a) – Motion to determine whether a sentenced person is suffering from a mental disease or defect and needs mental health treatment.	The defendant may be committed for a reasonable time (not to exceed 30 days) for examination; the court may approve a 15-day extension. The examination will be conducted at the nearest suitable facility to the court, if practicable.	
§ 4245(d) - Commitment of a person who is presently suffering from a mental disease or defect for the treatment of which he is in need of custody for care or treatment in a suitable facility.	The defendant shall be committed to the custody of the Attorney General for hospitalization until the offender is no longer in need of custody or until the expiration of the sentence of imprisonment, whichever occurs earlier.	
§ 4246(a) - Certification of an inmate who is due for release but continues to suffer from mental disease or defect, and as a result, is dangerous.	The director of the facility may file a certificate with the court if, because of the person's mental condition, his or her release would create a substantial risk of bodily injury to others or serious damage to property of another.	

47

Statutory Section	Role of the Attorney General	Role of State/Local Government or Agencies
POST-TRIAL	**POST-TRIAL**	**POST-TRIAL**
§ 4246(d) – Civil commitment of an inmate who cannot be released because a mental condition creates risk of harm to others.	The inmate shall be committed until the State will assume responsibility for the inmate or the person's condition improves such that release would not create a substantial risk of bodily injury to another or serious damage to property of another. The Attorney General shall try to make arrangements for the State to assume responsibility for the inmate's care and treatment.	The State may agree to assume responsibility for the care and treatment of the person. The Attorney General may seek civil commitment under State law. See 18 U.S.C. § 4247(i)(B).
§ 4248 – Civil commitment of a sexually dangerous person.	The Bureau of Prisons may certify to the court that the person is a sexually dangerous person. The court shall order a hearing to make that determination. If after the hearing, the court finds by clear and convincing evidence that the person is sexually dangerous, the court shall commit the person to the custody of the Attorney General. The Attorney General shall try to make arrangements for the State to assume responsibility for the committee's care and treatment.	The State may agree to assume responsibility for the care and treatment of the person.

APPENDIX B: **Regional Counsel and Consolidated Legal Center Offices**

Mid-Atlantic Region - MARO:	**North Central Region - NCRO:**	**South Central Region - SCRO:**
Matthew Mellady, Regional Counsel Phone: 301-317-3120 Fax: 301-317-3132 Zachary Kelton, Deputy Regional Counsel Phone: 301-317-3113 Mid-Atlantic Regional Office 302 Sentinel Drive, Suite 200 Annapolis Junction, MD 20701	Richard W. Schott, Regional Counsel Phone: 913-551-1004 Fax: 913-551-1107 Rick Winter, Deputy Regional Counsel Phone: 913-551-1006 North Central Regional Office Gateway Complex Tower II, 8th Floor 4th and State Avenue Kansas City, KS 66101	Jason Sickler, Regional Counsel Phone: 972-730-8920 Fax: 972- 730- 8929 Michael Frazier, Deputy Regional Counsel Phone: 972-730-8921 South Central Regional Office U.S. Armed Forces Reserve Complex 344 Marine Forces Drive Grand Prairie, TX 75051
Northeast Region - NERO:	**Western Region - WXRO:**	**Southeast Region - SERO:**
Michael Tafelski, Regional Counsel Phone: 215-521-7375 Fax: 215-521-7483 Joyce Horikawa, Deputy Regional Counsel Phone: 215-521-7376 Northeast Regional Office U.S. Custom House - 7th Floor 2nd and Chestnut Streets Philadelphia, PA 19106	Dennis Wong, Regional Counsel Phone: 209-956-9732 Fax: 209-956-9795 Dominic Ayotte, Deputy Regional Counsel Phone: 209-956-9731 Western Regional Office 7338 Shoreline Drive Stockton, CA 95219	Lisa Sunderman, Regional Counsel Phone: 678-686-1260 Fax: 678-686-1299 Craig Simmons, Deputy Regional Counsel Phone: 678-686-1281 Southeast Regional Office 3800 Camp Creek Parkway, SW Building 2000 Atlanta, GA 30331-6226

Consolidated Legal Centers

• = CLC LEADER   * = NOT ACTIVATED

MARO	NERO	NCRO	WXRO	SCRO/Dallas	SERO
• Zachary Kelton 301-317-3113	• Joyce Horikawa 215-521-7378	• Rick Winter 913-551-1006	• Dominic Ayotte 209-956-9731	• Michael D. Frazier 972-730-8921	• Craig Simmons 678-686-1281
FCI Cumberland, MD FCI Morgantown, WV FCI Memphis, TN FCC Hazelton, WV	FDC Philadelphia, PA FCI Fort Dix, NJ FCI Fairton, NJ FCI McKean, PA FCI Elkton, OH FCI Loretto, PA USP Canaan, PA Contract: Youngstown, OH Phillipsburg, PA	USP Leavenworth, KS USMCFP Springfield, MO	FCI Dublin, CA MCC San Diego USP Atwater, CA FDC Honolulu, HI FCI, Herlong, CA FCI Sheridan, OR FCI Mendota, CA FDC SeaTac, WA USP Atwater, CA Contract: TCI Taft, CA	FCI Ft. Worth, TX FMC Carswell, TX FCI La Tuna, TX FSI La Tuna, TX FCI Big Spring, TX FCI Seagoville, TX Contract: Big Spring, TX Eden, TX Milan, NM Post, TX Pecos, TX Raymondville, TX	FCI Talladega, AL FCI Jesup, GA MDC Guaynabo, PR Contract: McCrae, GA Folkston, GA

FMC Lexington	MCC New York	FMC Rochester	FCI Phoenix	FDC Houston	FCC Coleman
• Carlos Javier Martinez 859-255-6812 x5710	• Adam Johnson 646-836-6455	• VACANT 507-424-7445	• David Huband 623-465-9757 x4378	• Eric Hammonds 713-229-4104	• Jeffrey Middendorf 352-689-7382
FMC Lexington, KY FCI Ashland, KY FCI Manchester, KY USP Big Sandy, KY USP McCreary, KY	MCC New York, NY MDC Brooklyn, NY FCI Otisville, NY	FMC Rochester, MN FPC Duluth, MN FCI Sandstone, MN FCI Waseca, MN FPC Yankton, SD	FCI Phoenix, AZ FCC Tucson, AZ (2) FCI Safford, AZ	FCI Bastrop, TX FCI Three Rivers, TX FDC Houston, TX USP Pollock, LA FCI Pollock, LA FCC Oakdale, LA (2)	FCC Coleman, FL

Consolidated Legal Centers
• = CLC LEADER   * = NOT ACTIVATED

FCI Beckley	FCC Allenwood	St. Louis, MO	MDC Los Angeles	FCC Beaumont	FDC Miami
• Debbie Stevens 304-252-9758 x4105 FCI Beckley, WV FPC Alderson, WV USP Lee, VA FCI McDowell, WV FCI Gilmer, WV	• Lori Cunningham 570-522-7642 FCC Allenwood, PA USP Lewisburg, PA FCI Schuylkill, PA	• Paul Pepper 314-539-2382 MCC Chicago, IL FCI Oxford, WI FCI Pekin, IL USP Marion, IL FCI Greenville, IL FCI Terre Haute, IN USP Terre Haute, IN FCI Milan, MI *USP Thomson, IL	• Eliezer Ben-Shmuel 213-485-0439 x5428 MDC Los Angeles, CA FCI Terminal Island, CA FCC Lompoc, CA FCC Victorville, CA	• Juliana Reese-Colson 409-727-8187 x3262 FCC Beaumont, TX FPC Bryan, TX	• Rick DeAguiar 305-259-2511 FDC Miami, FL FCI Miami, FL FCI Tallahassee, FL FCI Marianna, FL FPC Pensacola, FL

FMC Butner	FMC Devens	FCC Florence		FTC Oklahoma City	SC/FCI Edgefield
• Mike Bredenberg 919-575-3900 x6078 FMC Butner, NC FCI I Butner, NC FCI Butner, NC FCI II Butner NC LSCI Butner, NC FCI I Petersburg, VA FCI II Petersburg, VA Contract: Winton, NC	• Les Owen 978-796-1043 FCI Danbury, CT FCI Ray Brook, NY FMC Devens, MA FCI Berlin, NH	• Chris Synsvoll 719-784-5216 FCI Florence, CO USP Florence, CO ADMAX Florence, CO FPC Florence, CO FCI Englewood, CO		• J. D. Crook 405-680-4004 FTC Oklahoma City, OK FCC Forrest City, AR (2) FCI Texarkana, TX FCI El Reno, OK	• Tami Rippon Cassaro 803-637-1307 FCI Edgefield, SC FCI Estill, SC FCI Williamsburg, SC FCI Bennettsville, SC

APPENDIX C: Relevant Acronyms and Abbreviations

A&O	Admission and Orientation
AOUSC	Administrative Office of the U.S. Courts
APA	Administrative Procedures Act
BOP	Federal Bureau of Prisons
CCC	Community Corrections Center
CCM	Community Corrections Manager
CMP	Correctional Management Plan
CMU	Communication Management Unit
CIMS	Central Inmate Monitoring System
COIF	Cost of Incarceration Fee
CRP	Certification Review Panel
CSC	Comprehensive Sanctions Center
CTP	Commitment Treatment Program
D.C.	District of Columbia
DOJ	United States Department of Justice
DHO	Discipline Hearing Officer
DSCC	Designation and Sentence Computation Center
ESL	English as a Second Language
FCC	Federal Correctional Complex
FCI	Federal Correctional Institution
FDC	Federal Detention Center
FMC	Federal Medical Center
FOIA	Freedom of Information Act
FPC	Federal Prison Camp
FPI	Federal Prison Industries
FTC	Federal Transfer Center
GCT	Good Conduct Time
GED	General Educational Development
HHS	Health and Human Services
IAC	Inmate Accident Compensation
IAD	Interstate Agreement on Detainers
ICC	Intensive Confinement Center
ICE	U.S. Immigration and Customs Enforcement
IFRP	Inmate Financial Responsibility Program
ISM	Inmate Systems Management
J&C	Judgment and Commitment Order
JCAHO	Joint Commission on the Accreditation of Healthcare Organizations
JJDPA	Federal Juvenile Justice and Delinquency Prevention Act
JPATS	Justice Prisoner and Alien Transportation System
MARO	Mid-Atlantic Regional Office, Bureau of Prisons

MCFP	Medical Center for Federal Prisoners
MCC	Metropolitan Correctional Center
MDC	Metropolitan Detention Center
MINT	Mothers and Infants Together
MVRA	Mandatory Victims Restitution Act
NERO	Northeast Regional Office, Bureau of Prisons
NCRO	North Central Regional Office, Bureau of Prisons
OMDT	Office of Medical Designations and Transportation
PREA	Prison Rape Elimination Act
PSF	Public Safety Factor
PSR	Presentence Report
PLRA	Prison Litigation Reform Act of 1995
RDAP	Residential Drug Abuse Program
RIVES	Reduction in Sentence
RRC	Residential Reentry Center
RRM	Residential Reentry Management Branch
SAM	Special Administrative Measure
SDP	Sexually Dangerous Person
SCRO	South Central Regional Office, Bureau of Prisons
SERO	Southeast Regional Office, Bureau of Prisons
SGT	Statutory Good Time
SHU	Special Housing Unit
SIS	Special Investigative Supervisor
SMU	Special Management Unit
SOR	Statement of Reasons
SORC	Sex Offender Release Coordinator
SOMP	Sex Offender Management Program
SORNA	Sex Offender Reporting and Notification Act
SOTP	Sex Offender Treatment Program
TRULINCS	Trust Fund Limited Inmate Computer System
UDC	Unit Discipline Committee
UNICOR	Federal Prison Industries trade name
USSG	United States Sentencing Guidelines
USMS	United States Marshals Service
USP	United States Penitentiary
USPO	United States Probation Office
VCCLEA	Violent Crime Control and Law Enforcement Act of 1994
WXRO	Western Region, Bureau of Prisons